Making the Familiar Unfamiliar

Zygmunt Bauman

Making the Familiar Unfamiliar

A Conversation with Peter Haffner

Translated by Daniel Steuer

polity

This English edition © 2020 by Polity Press

The translation of this work was supported by a grant from the Goethe-Institut.

Polity Press
65 Bridge Street
Cambridge CB2 1UR, UK

Polity Press
101 Station Landing
Suite 300
Medford, MA 02155, USA

ISBN-13: 978-1-5095-4230-7
ISBN-13: 978-1-5095-4231-4 (paperback)

A catalogue record for this book is available from the British Library.

Library of Congress Cataloging-in-Publication Data

Names: Bauman, Zygmunt, 1925-2017, interviewee. | Haffner, Peter, 1953-interviewer.
Title: Making the familiar unfamiliar : a conversation with Peter Haffner / Zygmunt Bauman ; translated by Daniel Steuer.
Other titles: Vertraute unvertraut machen. English.
Description: Cambridge, UK ; Medford, MA : Polity Press, 2020. | Includes bibliographical references. | Summary: "The last interview of one of the greatest social thinkers of our time"-- Provided by publisher.
Identifiers: LCCN 2020012868 (print) | LCCN 2020012869 (ebook) | ISBN 9781509542307 (hardback) | ISBN 9781509542314 (paperback) | ISBN 9781509542321 (epub)
Subjects: LCSH: Bauman, Zygmunt, 1925-2017--Interviews. | Sociologists--Poland--Interviews. | Civilization, Modern--20th century. | Sociology--Philosophy.
Classification: LCC HM479.B39 A5 2020 (print) | LCC HM479.B39 (ebook) | DDC 301.092--dc23
LC record available at https://lccn.loc.gov/2020012868
LC ebook record available at https://lccn.loc.gov/2020012869

Typeset in 11 on 13pt Sabon
by Fakenham Prepress Solutions, Fakenham, N orfolk NR21 8NL
Printed and bound in Great Britain by CPI Group (UK) Ltd, Croydon

For further information on Polity, visit our website:
politybooks.com

Contents

Editorial Note   vii
Preface   viii

Love and Gender   1
Choosing a partner: why we are losing the capacity to love

Experience and Remembrance   9
Fate: how we make the history that makes us

Jewishness and Ambivalence   26
Adaptation: why were Jews attracted to communism?

Intellect and Commitment   40
Sociology: why it should not separate objective from personal
experience

Power and Identity   52
Modernity: on the compulsion to be no one, or
become someone else

Society and Responsibility   67
Solidarity: why everyone becomes everyone else's enemy

Religion and Fundamentalism   87
The end of the world: why it is important to believe
in (a non-existent) God

Utopia and History   99
Time travel: where is 'the beyond' today?

Present and Future   107
Human waste: who are the witches of modern society?

Happiness and Morality   122
The good life: what does it mean to take off shoes that are
too tight?

Translator's notes   132
Select bibliography   135

Editorial Note

The conversations with Zygmunt Bauman that form the basis of this book took place on 10 February 2014 and 21–23 April 2016 at his home in Leeds, England. In addition, Bauman provided me with notes containing biographical information and thoughts on various topics, as well as with excerpts from his then forthcoming book *Retrotopia*, and he asked me to make use of certain passages of these written sources as answers to some of my questions, so that he would not need to repeat himself in conversation. He also asked me to make use, at one point, of his answers to two questions that had been put to him in an interview conducted by Efrain Kristal and Arne De Boever and published under the title 'Disconnecting Acts' in the *Los Angeles Review of Books* of 11/12 November 2014. In total, the passages based on all these written sources amount to about a dozen pages of the text.

My 2014 interview appeared on 4 July 2015 under the title 'Die Welt, in der wir leben' [The world we live in] in *Das Magazin* (the Saturday supplement of *Tages-Anzeiger*, *Basler Zeitung*, *Berner Zeitung* and *Der Bund*).

Peter Haffner

Preface

When I visited Zygmunt Bauman for the first time, I was astonished by what seemed a contradiction between the person and his work. Arguably the most influential European sociologist, someone whose anger about the state of the world can be felt in his every line, Bauman enchanted me with his wry sense of humour. His charm was disarming, his *joie de vivre* infectious.

Following his retirement from the University of Leeds in 1990, Zygmunt Bauman had published book after book at an almost alarming pace. The themes of these books stretch from intimacy to globalization, from reality TV to the Holocaust, from consumerism to cyberspace. He has been called the 'head of the anti-globalization movement', the 'leader of the Occupy movement' and the 'prophet of postmodernism'. He is read the world over and considered a truly exceptional scholar in the field of the humanities, whose fragmentation into separate, sharply delineated and jealously protected areas of research he ignored with the insatiable curiosity of a Renaissance man. His reflections do not distinguish between the political and the personal. Why we have lost the capacity to love, why we find it hard to make moral judgements: he investigates the social and personal aspects of these questions with the same thoroughness.

It was this epic view of the world that fascinated me when I began to read his books. It is impossible to remain indifferent to what Zygmunt Bauman writes, even if one does not agree with one or other of the points he makes – or, indeed, even if one disagrees with him altogether. Whoever engages with his work comes away viewing the world, and him- or herself, differently. Zygmunt Bauman described his task as that of making the familiar unfamiliar and the unfamiliar familiar. This, he said, is the task of sociology as such.

This task can only be approached by someone who has the whole human being in view and who moves beyond his or her particular discipline and into philosophy, psychology, anthropology and history, art and literature. Zygmunt Bauman is not someone for minute details, statistical analyses and polls, figures, facts or projections. He draws his pictures with a broad brush on a large canvas, formulates claims, introduces new theses into discussions and provokes disputes. In terms of Isaiah Berlin's famous typology of thinkers and writers – based on the dictum of the Greek poet Archilochos that 'The fox knows many things, but the hedgehog knows *one* big thing' – Zygmunt Bauman is both hedgehog and fox.[1] He introduced the concept of 'liquid modernity' to describe our present times, wherein all aspects of life – love, friendship, work, leisure, family, community, society, religion, politics and power – are transformed at unprecedented speed. 'My life is spent recycling information', he once said. That sounds modest until one appreciates the amount of material involved.

In a time marked by fear and insecurity, when many people are being taken in by the simple solutions offered by populism, critical analysis of the problems and contradictions in society and the world is needed more than ever. Such analysis is an essential precondition if we are to be able to think about alternatives, even if these are not within easy reach. Zygmunt Bauman, erstwhile communist, never stopped believing in the possibility of a better society, despite all the dreams that have failed. His interest was never in the winners, but in the losers, the uprooted and disenfranchised, the growing numbers of the underprivileged – not only poor people of colour in the Global South, but also members of the Western workforce. The fear that the ground that seemed rock solid during the good old post-war years is giving way is today a global phenomenon, and the middle classes are not spared from it. In a climate that asks you to accept the given and to understand the world, following Leibniz, as the best of all possible worlds, Zygmunt Bauman defends the moment of utopia – not as a blueprint for some future castle in the air but as a motivation to improve the conditions under which we live here and now.

Zygmunt Bauman welcomed me to his house in Leeds, England, for four long conversations on his life's work. The enchanting front garden, with its moss-covered chairs and its table overgrown by shrubs, borders on a busy road, as if to illustrate that it is only through contradiction that things become fully clear. At 90 years of age, Zygmunt Bauman was tall, slim and as lively and perspicacious as ever. He accompanied his deliberations with extensive gesticulation, as if he were a conductor; in order to emphasize a point, he slammed his fist down on his armrest. When talking about the prospect of dying, he did so with the composure of someone who, as a soldier in the Second World War, a Polish Jew, a refugee in Soviet Russia and a victim of the anti-Semitic purge of Poland in 1968, had experienced at first hand the dark side of the 'liquid modernity' whose theoretician he had become.

On each occasion, the coffee table was overloaded with croissants and biscuits, canapés and fruit tarts, cookies and crab mousse, accompanied by hot and cold drinks, juices and Polish 'kompot'. While my host shared his thoughts with me, he also never forgot to remind me to help myself to all the delights that had been set out in front of me.

Zygmunt Bauman talked about life and the attempts to shape it that are consistently thwarted by fate; he spoke also about the effort to remain, amid all this, someone who can look at himself in the mirror. His hope for me, he said, grasping both my hands as he bade me farewell, was that I would live to be as old as him, because every age, despite all its tribulations, has its beauty.

Zygmunt Bauman died on 9 January 2017 at his home in Leeds.

These final conversations with Bauman will, I hope, be taken up and continued by the reader with other people and in other places.

Peter Haffner, January 2017

Love and Gender

Choosing a partner: why we are losing the capacity to love

Let us begin with the most important thing: love. You say that we are losing the capacity to love. What brings you to that conclusion?

The trend of looking for partners on the internet follows the trend towards internet shopping. I myself do not like to go to shops; most things, such as books, films, clothes, I buy online. If you want a new jacket, the website of the online shop shows you a catalogue. If you are looking for a new partner, the dating website also shows you a catalogue. The pattern of relationships between customer and commodity becomes the pattern of relationships between human beings.

How is this different from earlier times, when you met your future life companion at the village fete or, if you lived in a city, at a ball? There were personal preferences involved in that as well, weren't there?

For people who are shy, the internet is certainly helpful. They do not have to worry about blushing when they approach a woman. It is easier for them to make a connection; they are less inhibited. But online dating is about attempting to define the partner's properties in accordance with one's own desires. The partner is chosen according to hair colour, height, build, chest measurement, age, and their interests, hobbies, preferences and aversions. This is based on the idea that the object of love can be assembled out of a number of measurable physical and social properties. We lose sight of the decisive factor: the human person.

But even if one defines one's 'type' in this way, isn't it the case that everything changes as soon as one meets the actual person? That person, after all, is much more than the sum of such external properties.

The danger is that the form of human relationships assumes the form of the relationship one has towards the objects of daily use. I do not vow to be faithful to a chair – why should I vow that I shall keep this as my chair until my dying day? If I do not like it any longer, I buy a new one. This is not a conscious process, but we learn to see the world and human beings in this way. What happens when we meet someone who is more attractive? It is like the case of the Barbie doll: once a new version is on the market, the old one is exchanged for it.

You mean, we separate prematurely?

We enter into a relationship because we expect satisfaction from it. If we feel that another person will give us more satisfaction, we end the current relationship and begin a new one. The beginning of a relationship requires an agreement between two people; ending it only takes one person. This means that both partners live in constant fear of being abandoned, of being discarded like a jacket that has fallen out of fashion.

Well, that is part of the nature of any agreement.

Sure. But in earlier times it was almost impossible to break off a relationship, even if it was not satisfying. Divorce was difficult, and alternatives to marriage practically non-existent. You suffered, yet you stayed together.

And why would the freedom to separate be worse than the compulsion to stay together and be unhappy?

You gain something but also lose something. You have more freedom, but you suffer from the fact that your partner also has more freedom. This leads to a life in which relationships and partnerships are formed on the model of hire purchase. Someone who can leave ties behind does not need to make an effort to preserve them. Human beings are only considered valuable as long as they provide satisfaction. This is based on the belief that lasting ties get in the way of the quest for happiness.

And that, as you say in Liquid Love, *your book on friendship and relationships, is erroneous.*

It is the problem of 'liquid love'. In turbulent times, you need friends and partners who do not let you down, who are there for you when you need them. The desire for stability is important in life. The 16-billion-dollar valuation for Facebook is based on that need not to be alone. But, at the same time, we dread the commitment of becoming involved with someone and getting tied down. The fear is that of missing out on something. You want a safe harbour, but at the same time you want to have a free hand.

For sixty-one years you were married to Janina Lewinson, who died in 2009. In her memoir, A Dream of Belonging, *she writes that, after your first encounter, you never left her side. Each time, you exclaimed 'what a happy coincidence'*

*it was that you had to go where she wanted to go! And
when she told you that she was pregnant, you danced in
the street and kissed her – while wearing your Polish Army
captain's uniform, which caused something of a stir. Even
after decades of marriage, Janina writes, you still sent her
love letters. What constitutes true love?*

When I saw Janina, I knew at once that I did not need
to look further. It was love at first sight. Within nine
days I had proposed to her. True love is that elusive but
overwhelming joy of the 'I and thou', being there for one
another, becoming one, the joy of making a difference in
something that is important not only to you. To be needed,
or even perhaps irreplaceable, is an exhilarating feeling. It
is difficult to achieve. And it is unattainable if you remain in
the solitude of the egotist who is only interested in himself.

Love demands sacrifice, then.

If the nature of love consists in the inclination always
to stand by the object of your love, to support it, to
encourage and praise it, then a lover must be prepared
to put self-interest in second place, behind the loved one
– must be prepared to consider his or her own happiness
as a side-issue, a side-effect of the happiness of the other.
To use the Greek poet Lucian's words, the beloved is the
one to whom one 'pledges one's fate'. Contrary to the
prevailing wisdom, within a loving relationship, altruism
and egotism are not irreconcilable opposites. They unite,
amalgamate and finally can no longer be distinguished or
separated from each other.

*The American writer Colette Dowling dubbed women's
fear of independence the 'Cinderella complex'. She calls
the yearning for security, warmth and being-cared-for
a 'dangerous emotion' and urges her fellow women not
to deprive themselves of their freedom. Where do you
disagree with this admonition?*

Dowling warned against the impulse to care for others and thus to lose the possibility of jumping, at will, on the latest bandwagon. It is typical of the private utopias of the cowboys and cowgirls of the consumer age that they demand an enormous degree of freedom for themselves. They think the world revolves around them, and the performances they aim for are solo acts. They can never get enough of that.

The Switzerland in which I grew up was not a democracy. Until 1971, women – that is, half of the population – did not have the vote. The principle of equal pay for equal work is still not established, and women are under-represented in boardrooms. Are there not any number of good reasons for women to get rid of their dependencies?

Equal rights in these areas are important. But there are two movements within feminism that must be distinguished. One of them wants to make women indistinguishable from men. Women are meant to serve in the army and go to war, and they ask: why are we not allowed to shoot other people dead when men are permitted to do so? The other movement wants to make the world more feminine. The military, politics, everything that has been created, was created by men for men. A lot of what is wrong today is the result of that fact. Equal rights – of course. But should women simply pursue the values that have been created by men?

Is this not a decision that, in a democracy, must be left to women themselves?

Well, in any case, I do not expect that the world would be very much better if women functioned the same way that men did and do.

In the early years of your marriage you were a house-husband avant la lettre. *You did the cooking and looked after two little children while your wife worked in an office. That was rather unusual in the Poland of those days, wasn't it?*

It wasn't all that unusual, even though Poland was a conservative country. In that respect, the communists were revolutionary, because they considered men and women to be equal as workers. The novelty about communist Poland was that a large number of women worked in factories or offices. You needed two incomes at the time in order to provide for a family.

That led to a change in the position of women and thus to a change in relations between the sexes.

It was an interesting phenomenon. The women tried to understand themselves as economic agents. In the old Poland, the husband had been the sole provider, responsible for the whole family. In fact, however, women made an enormous contribution to the economy. Women took care of a lot of the work, but it did not count and was not translated into economic value. Just to give an example, when the first laundrette opened in Poland, making it possible to have someone else wash one's dirty laundry, this saved people an enormous amount of time. I remember that my mother spent two days a week doing the washing, drying and ironing for the whole family. But women were reluctant to make use of the new service. Journalists wanted to know why. They told the women that having someone else do their laundry was much cheaper than them doing it themselves. 'How come?', the women exclaimed, presenting the journalists with a calculation showing that the overall cost of washing powder, soap and fuel for the stoves used for heating up the water was lower than that of having everything washed at the laundrette. But they had not included their labour in the calculation. The idea that their labour also had its price did not occur to them.

That was no different in the West.

It took several years before society got used to the fact that the household work done by women also had a price tag attached. But by the time people had become aware of this, there were soon only very few families with traditional housewives.

In her memoirs, Janina writes that you took care of everything when she fell ill with puerperal fever after the birth of your twin daughters. You got up at night when the babies, Lydia and Irena, were crying, gave them a bottle; you changed nappies, washed them in the morning and hung them up to dry in the backyard. You took Anna, your oldest daughter, to the nursery, fetched her again. You waited in the long queues in front of the shops when doing the errands. And you did all this while also fulfilling your duties as a lecturer, supervising your students, writing your own dissertation and attending political meetings. How did you manage to do that?

As was the norm in academic life back then, I was more or less able to dispose of my time as I chose. I went to the university when I had to, to give a seminar or a lecture. Apart from that, I was a free man. I could stay in my office or go home, go for walks, dance, do whatever I liked. Janina, by comparison, worked in an office. She reviewed screenplays; she was a translator and editor at the Polish state-run film company. There was a time clock there, and it was thus clear that I had to be there for the children and the housework whenever she was at the office or ill. That did not lead to any tension; it was taken for granted.

Janina and you grew up in different circumstances. She came from a wealthy family of physicians; in your family, money was always tight. And Janina was probably not prepared for being a housewife, for cooking, cleaning, doing all the work that in her parents' home had been done by servants.

I grew up in the kitchen. Cooking was routine work for me. Janina cooked when it was necessary. She followed recipes, with a cookbook in front of her – terribly boring. That is why she did not like it. I observed my mother every day working miracles at the cooker, creating something out of nothing. We had little money, and she was able to produce a tasty meal even out of the worst raw ingredients. In this way, I naturally acquired the skill of cookery. It is not a talent, and neither was I taught it. I simply watched how it was done.

Janina said of you that you are the 'Jewish mother'. You still love to cook today, even though you do not have to.

I love it because cooking is creative. I have come to realize that what you do in the kitchen resembles very much what you do at the computer when you write: you create something. It is creative work: interesting, not boring. What's more, a good couple is not a combination of two identical people. A good couple is one where the partners complement each other. What one of them lacks, the other possesses. That was the case with Janina and me. She did not like cooking very much; I did – and thus we complemented each other.

Experience and Remembrance
Fate: how we make the history that makes us

In 1946, you joined the Polish Workers' Party (PPR), the communist party of Poland. That was one year before Leszek Kołakowski, the philosopher who taught at All Souls College, Oxford, and died in 2009. In 1968, you left the party, Kołakowski having been excluded two years earlier. In contrast to you, he later became a self-declared anti-Marxist.

Kołakowski and I did not co-ordinate our joining of the communist party. We did not yet know of each other; we hadn't yet met. When in retrospect we tried to recall our feelings at the time, first in Poland, then in exile, and finally after the fall of the Berlin Wall in 1989, we agreed on one point: we had both believed that the programme of the Polish communists in 1944/5 was the only one that gave us some reason to hope that our country could escape from the backwardness of the pre-war era and the cataclysm of the war; that it was the only programme that could solve the nation's problems of moral degeneration, illiteracy, poverty and social injustice. The communists wanted to give land to impoverished farmers, improve the living conditions of the workers in the factories, nation-alize industry. They wanted to provide universal education – and that promise they actually kept. There was a revolution in education, and, despite all the economic nepotism, culture flourished: Polish film, Polish theatre and Polish literature were first class. That is no longer the case in Poland today. In my little book *The Art of Life* ...

A wonderful book, my favourite book of yours...

... in this book I elaborate on the idea that the journey of human life is based on two interacting factors. One is fate. 'Fate' is a shorthand for those things over which we have no control. And the other factor is the realistic options made possible by fate. A girl from New York born in Harlem has a different fate from a girl born near Central Park. The sets of options they have differ.

But both have such a set, have a choice. What then deter-mines which possibilities someone tries to realize?

Character. We cannot escape the set of realistic options that fate presents to us, but different people will make different choices, and that is a question of character. That is why there is just as much reason for pessimism as there is for optimism: pessimism, because there are insuperable limits to the possibilities open to us, which is what we call fate; and optimism because we can work on our character in a way that we cannot on our fate. I bear no responsibility for my fate; that is God's decision, if you like. But I bear responsibility for my character, because it is something that can be formed, purified and improved.

What did that look like in your case?

My own journey, like any other, was a combination of fate and character. I could not do anything about my fate. As far as my character is concerned, I do not pretend that it is perfect, but I take responsibility for every decision I have made. That is irreversible. I did what I did, and fate alone is not enough to explain it.

Looking back at your life, what would you do differently?

What would I do differently? Oh no, I do not answer that kind of question.

Okay.

What would I do differently? When I was still very young, still a little boy, I wrote a novel, a biography of Hadrian, the Roman emperor. During my research, I came across a sentence I have never forgotten. That sentence is about the senselessness of reflection on questions such as 'What would you have done differently?' It runs: 'If the Trojan Horse had offspring, the keeping of horses would be very cheap.'

The power and impotence of the little word 'if'.

The point, of course, is that the Trojan Horse could not have had offspring because it was made of wood. That is the answer to the question of what I would have done differently. How would the subsequent course of history have been changed if you had done something differently? I do not attach any particular importance to my own decisions. They were taken within the logic of the times. Very important changes in my life happened without me having anything to do with it, without me taking the initiative. That I had to flee from Poznań, had to leave Poland when the Nazis arrived, was down to neither my desire nor my will. What I did decide myself was to join the communist party after the war. Given the circumstances at the time, and given my own experience, that was the best thing I could think of and could do. I was not alone in this belief, and many of those who later became

ardent anti-communists took the same decision I took –
including, for instance, Leszek Kołakowski.

*Janina, who joined the communist party under your
influence, describes her shock when she found out that
information about one of her female colleagues which
she had passed on to a comrade had led to her colleague
being ostracized. You explained to her, she says, that the
party, despite being 'still full of untrustworthy individuals,
ruthless careerists, and immature members', was 'the
strongest force for social justice'. It was impossible 'to make
a revolution without inadvertently damaging innocent
people'. Later, neither Kołakowski nor you sought to hide
behind such justifications.*

Our individual processes of disenchantment, the slowly yet
inexorably dawning awareness of the abyss that separates
theory and practice, and the realization of the pathological
moral effects of the hypocrisy that was associated with it,
took place more or less in parallel. Except for one thing: the
illusion that the party might still have been brought back on
to the right path, the path from which it had strayed – that
its crude mistakes might have been rectified from within.
To that illusion I succumbed for one or two years longer
than Leszek, a fact of which I still feel ashamed. Later, in
exile, our attitudes diverged widely, though. In contrast to
Leszek, I never joined the opposite political camp, let alone
showed any enthusiasm for it. I am still a socialist.

*You were a soldier in the Polish division of the Red
Army, and after the war an officer in the Korpus
Bezpieczeństwa Wewnętrznego (KBW), the Internal
Security Corps. Apart from the military training, was
there also political education, or, as one might have to
say, indoctrination?*

As long as the war against the German occupiers continued,
there was very little of that. The only aim was to end the

occupation, and what would become of Poland afterwards remained a matter of minor importance. That changed once the military operations ended. The soldiers of the KBW represented a cross-section of the population. Thus, the perspectives and preferences differed, reflecting the schisms within Polish society. Apart from the usual virtues of the soldier, the main theme of the political instruction was the still open question of 'Which Poland do the Polish need most urgently?' 'Marxism–Leninism versus bourgeois philosophy' might have been the main theme within the academic world, but among soldiers the questions were 'Who owns the factories?' and 'Who owns the arable land?'

In 2007, the German-Polish historian Bogdan Musiał attacked you on the grounds of your membership of the KBW, but he did not find any evidence that you were involved in murder, torture or spying on anti-communist partisans, activities of which the KBW has been accused.

The things that are true in Musiał's *Frankfurter Allgemeine Zeitung* article are not news. Everyone knew that I had been a communist between 1946 and 1967, and also that I had served in the so-called 'internal army' for several years.[2] What his article did reveal was only that I also worked for the military intelligence service. I was 19 years old at the time, and I only did this for three years. I had never made this public because I had signed a document that committed me to keeping it secret.

What was your task, then?

Nothing special: dull office work. I was in the division for propaganda and agitation. I had to prepare material for the theoretical and practical education of conscripts, had to compose ideological pamphlets. Luckily, for me, this soon came to an end.

A protocol quoted by Musiał says, of the 'informant Semjon', which was your code name: 'His information is valuable. Due to his Semitic origin, he can't be used for operative work.' Was it your task to collect information on enemies of the regime?

That was probably expected of me, but I can't remember having provided anything of that nature. I was sitting, writing, in an office – not exactly the sort of place where you come by such information. What Musiał does not say is that, while I might have worked for three years for military intelligence, I was myself monitored by the secret service for fifteen years. I was spied upon, reports were written on me, my telephone was tapped, my flat bugged and so on. Because I was a critic of the regime, I was thrown out of the army, and then out of the university, and thus out of Poland.

After the Hungarian Uprisings of 1956, you were among the rebels in the party. Janina describes how you and your family were pursued and mistreated. In order to marry her, you needed the permission of your military superior, Colonel Zdzisław Bibrowski. Like yourself, he was a communist, but apparently he was, likewise, not loyal to the party line.

From Bibrowski, I learned how to distinguish between healthy social bodies and cancerous outgrowths. He opened my eyes to the yawning gap between the socialist idea, to which I was committed with all my heart, and 'actually existing socialism', with which I had severe difficulties long before the GDR dissident Rudolf Bahro coined the phrase in 1977, and also long before I was forced to leave Poland. Bibrowski showed me that being loyal to the idea of socialism demands that you fight tooth and nail against it being watered down or corrupted. Once I had learned this lesson, I never forgot it.

Janina writes that Bibrowski was removed from his post in 1952 because he was a Jew.

I suspect that, sooner or later, he would have had to go anyhow because of his views. He was an intellectual of the highest calibre, a man with an open and critical mind who gathered around him young officers with similar qualities and protected them against the 'cleansing'. He was considered unsuitable in the context of the rapid professionalization of the state security service. Bibrowski was not an anti-communist – quite the opposite. He rebelled in the name of his belief, of communism, against its abuse, against it being spoiled and perverted. He was a man who wanted to serve the regime as well as preserve his own humanity and, thus, protect the humanity of others. But: *Amicus Plato, sed magis amica veritas*, as the saying ascribed to Aristotle has it. I love Plato, but I love truth even more. Bibrowski returned to his profession as an engineer. Shortly afterwards, the small group he had taken under his wing followed his example, I among them.

And you did not do so voluntarily, either. In January 1953, you were judged politically unreliable and dismissed from the army. Two months later, Joseph Stalin died. At the time he was admired as a 'great man', even in the West, someone – as Janina recalls – 'whose iron fist had crushed the Fascist ogre'.[3] How did you experience Stalin's death?

The shock was enormous. After all, I, and many others who were much smarter than me, had lived for thirteen years in the vast shadow cast by this man – had by and large trusted his wisdom and relied on his judgement. Until the present day, despite all we now know about the psychology of totalitarianism, I find it difficult fully to comprehend this intellectual suffocation. Volumes have been written about the cult surrounding Stalin and Hitler. The phenomenon has been described in minute detail and has widely been recognized as hopelessly incomprehensible.

If you want to become familiar with the experiences of this type of personality cult, you can do far worse than reading *Secondhand Time* by the Nobel Prize-winner Svetlana Alexievich. Although she is not exactly able to provide an explanation, she nevertheless comes closest to capturing the phenomenon. She lays bare the enigma, and provides a glimpse of its complexity for people who did not experience it themselves. Apart from that, I am currently haunted by the nightmare that such a cult may become fashionable again in the not all too distant future.

To what extent were you attracted by Marxism as a theory, as a sophisticated intellectual structure?

I do not believe that any ideas about relations of production and forces of production, about value theory or the emancipation of the working class, and the like, played a decisive role in my turn towards communism. I did not enter into it through the door of philosophy or political economy. Rather, it was a matter of an understanding of the present situation that combined with a romantic, rebellious vision of history and the role we, the young people, had to play: namely, to realize this vision. As Leszek put it so beautifully, in his essay 'The Death of Gods', we were fascinated by the 'myth of a Better World', by the dream of a 'kingdom of equality and freedom', the feeling of being 'brothers of the Paris communards, the workers during the Russian Revolution, the soldiers in the Spanish Civil War'.[4]

Janina's memoirs tell us that, after your removal from the army, the contradiction between the words and deeds of 'actually existing socialism' gave you the idea that, a hundred years after its inception, Marxist theory also needed to be given a new interpretation. What is your view today? What of Marx is still valid?

His analysis of the economic mechanisms is, of course, outdated. Marx was writing in the mid nineteenth century, in an entirely different situation. But he made many important observations that still guide me in my work. One of them, my favourite one, is the justification for sociology, its genuine *raison d'être*. Marx says: 'Men make their own history, but they do not make it just as they please in circumstances they choose for themselves; rather, they make it in present circumstances, given and inherited.'[5] This is the ground in which the existence of sociology as a science is rooted. You may spend your whole life fathoming this justification. The circumstances have been created, but we did not choose them. The question is how they emerged and what they force us to do, how we deal with them and how we can change them. How do we – under the pressures of contemporary conditions of life and in the knowledge of these conditions – consciously create history? That is the secret of our existence.

What does this mean for your kind of sociology in particular?

I was inspired, in particular, by what Antonio Gramsci, the Italian philosopher, Marxist and founder of Italy's communist party, did with this Marxian thought. I adopt the form of his approach, which I call sociological herme-neutics – which should not be confused with hermeneutic sociology as a school within sociology. What matters are the ideas that people accept, the guiding principles they follow. Sociological hermeneutics means reflecting on the conditions, the circumstances and the constitution of society. We are a natural species condemned to thinking, *Homo sapiens*; we experience something, do not just suffer it physically. Experiences are little pieces of information and disinformation from which we try to derive sense, create ideas, and out of which we try to make plans. Professional hermeneutics, by contrast, derives today's ideas from earlier ideas, interprets them on the basis of their past, uncovers how they multiply, create offspring, breed at will. But in my view, this is not how things proceed.

We must move on from the ideas to the body of society, and try to find the connection between the two. That is where the problem is located, the problem that divides us into different political factions, parties, affiliations and loyalties: the simple fact that the same experience can be interpreted in different ways. Gramsci's idea was that of a philosophy of hegemonic ideas, generally called common sense. The philosophy of hegemony is not philosophy in the sense of philosophical critique. It does not consist of disquisitions on Kant, Leibniz and such figures, but rather of what the Greeks called 'doxa', the 'considering true' of something – belief, as opposed to knowledge. Doxa are thoughts one does not think, but acts upon. They are sedimented somewhere, forming the framework of our perception of the world. Thanks to Gramsci, I spent the better part of my life deciphering the dominant and hegemonic ideas as reactions to the conditions of human life. I try to understand why neoliberalism suddenly becomes popular, or why there is a sudden return of the desire for strong leaders. For me, these are the challenges.

You were 18 when you joined General Berling's army in the Soviet Union and were sent to the frontline. What effects did the experience of war, of the devastation and destruction of your homeland, Poland, to which you returned, have on you? In the Soviet Union you had studied physics in your free time.

By the time I had returned with the Polish Army that had been formed in the USSR, my interest had already shifted from the natural to the social sciences. What I saw accelerated this process. Even before the German occupation, there had been great poverty in Poland. Many people were unemployed or underemployed; the social injustice was scandalous. After six years of German occupation, it was even worse. The people had been humiliated, the land scorched by the frontlines moving through it. It was no surprise, then, that I switched to social and political studies. After leaving the army, I dedicated myself fully to them.

The regiment of light artillery to which you belonged was positioned at the Weichsel outside Warsaw while the Russians waited until the Germans had crushed the uprising, killed 200,000 inhabitants, and laid the city to waste. In March 1945, you were wounded during the Battle of Kolberg, taken to a military hospital, and afterwards took part in the battle for Berlin. You were awarded the medal for bravery. For what, exactly?

I don't know. The medal was awarded to me while I was in the military hospital, and I only learned about it later, and at that point none of those who had nominated me could be contacted. All I can tell you is that I was in no way more courageous than hundreds of other Polish soldiers. I do not think that my participation in urban combat played a large role in the capture of Kolberg.

And the battle for Berlin?

I reached Berlin on 3 May, on foot, from the military hospital. Those were the very last days of fighting before Germany's capitulation on 8 May.

Did you learn anything during your military career that influenced your intellectual work?

Reconstructing my experiences of the 1940s runs the risk of violating Leopold von Ranke's demand that history should report 'how it actually was'. The only thing I am certain of is that I am never certain of whether I do really report how things actually were. The past is teeming with allusion and suggestion; it is a far more fruitful field for speculation than the future will ever be, even though the future lacks any points of orientation. Thus, what I say is how I see it at the present moment, but whether

I have succeeded in laying open the deepest layer of this palimpsest of subsequent sediments, I can neither know nor guarantee.

In concrete terms, did the military experiences you had as a young man, especially the liberation of Poland, influence your earliest ideas when you became a professor of sociology in Warsaw?

As the same question was put to me by the interviewers from the *Los Angeles Review of Books*, I repeat the answer I gave them, as published in 2014: 'They must have, mustn't they? How could it be otherwise? Be they military or civilian, life experiences cannot but imprint themselves – the more heavily the more acute they are – on life's trajectory, on the way we perceive the world, respond to it and pick the paths to walk through it. They combine into a matrix of which one's life's itinerary is one of the possible permutations. The point, though, is that they do their work silently, stealthily so to speak, and surreptitiously – by prodding rather than spurring, and through sets of options they circumscribe rather than through conscious, deliberate choices. Stanisław Lem, the great Polish story-teller as well as scientist, tried once, not entirely tongue in cheek, to compose an inventory of accidents leading to the birth of the person called "Stanisław Lem," and then calculate that birth's probability. He found that scientifically speaking his existence was well nigh impossible (though probability of other people's births – scoring no better than his – was also infinitely close to zero). And so a word of warning is in order: retrospectively reconstructing causes and motives of choices carries a danger of imputing structure to a flow, and logic – even predetermination – to what was in fact a series of *faits accomplis* poorly if at all reflected upon at the time of their happening... .

I recall here these mundane and rather trivial truths to warn you that what I am going to say in reply to your question needs to be taken with a pinch of salt... .

It "stands to reason" to connect the experiences during the war and the early post-war years with what were to become my lifelong academic interests: sources of evil, social inequality and its impact, roots and tools of injustice, virtues and vices of alternative modes of life, chances and limits of humans' control over their history. But is the quality of "standing to reason" a sufficient proof of being true? In his latest novel *Ostatnie Rozdanie*,[6] a book that apart from being a fascinating story told in an exquisite prose is also a long meditation on the traps and ambushes, trials and tribulations that cannot but lie in store for people cheeky and insolent enough to dare an orderly, comprehensive, and convincing reconstruction and retelling of their life itineraries, the formidable Polish writer Wiesław Myśliwski writes:

> I lived willy-nilly. Without any sense of being part of the order of things. I lived by fragments, pieces, scraps, in the moment, at random, from incident to incident, as if buffeted by ebb and flow. Oftentimes I had the impression that someone had torn the majority of pages out of the book of my life, because they were empty, or because they belonged not to me but to someone else's life.

But, he asks, "Someone will say: what about memory? Is it not a guardian of our selves? Does it not give us the feeling of being us, not someone else? Does it not make us whole, does it not brand us?" – only to answer: "Well, I would not advise putting trust in memory, since memory is at the mercy of our imagination, and as such cannot be a reliable source of truth about us." Humbly, I accept.

Martin Jay once opined that the liquidity of my own life experiences has influenced my interpretations of liquid modernity. Having been in my life story a bird rather than ornithologist (and birds are not known to be particularly prominent in the annals of ornithology), I really don't feel entitled to go beyond a rather banal observation that the experience of frailty of the settings in and through which I found myself moving must have (mustn't it?) influenced what I have seen and how I saw it.'[7]

Two weeks after the German invasion of Poland, your family fled to the Soviet Union, leaving on the last train. Almost thirty years later, you had to flee from Poland, your home, again. You first found refuge in Israel and then moved to Great Britain, where you stayed for good. Can you count the stages, the places of residence of this, your life's journey?

There are too many to list them all. In Warsaw, we lived in Prus Street 17, in a rented flat – my parents, my sister and I. Then we fled to Mołodeczno, which is today Maladziečna, Belarus, but at the time was occupied by the Red Army and, following the German–Soviet non-aggression pact, annexed to the Byelorussian Soviet Socialist Republic. There, we lived in one room of a farmhouse. In 1941, before the Germans captured the city, we fled to Shakhunya, a regional centre north of Gorki, today called Nizhny Novgorod again. We lived in a small, windowless room rented out by a widow. After the war, between 1948 and 1954, Janina, our oldest daughter, Anna, and I lived with my parents in a three-room flat in Sandomierska Street in Warsaw. After that, Janina and I moved into a two-room flat in aleja Zjednoczenia, and later to Nowotki Street, today's General Anders Street, where we stayed until we had to emigrate in 1968. After an intermezzo in Tel Aviv, I moved to Great Britain, to 1 Lawnswood Gardens, Leeds, where I shall also die. At first, I lived here with Janina, two of our daughters and the mother-in-law, then only with Janina, and today with my second wife, Aleksandra Jasińska-Kania.

In 1957, following the completion of your doctorate, you were awarded an American grant for a year of study at the

London School of Economics. You lived, Janina writes, in a dark, cold and damp room on a basement floor, lived off cheese and pasties, struggled with your English, and missed your family. You were sad, she says, felt terribly lonely, and you saved up money so that Janina could come and visit you.

Oh yes, I was despairing to begin with.

Then it got better, Janina reports. When she visited, she was surprised that the people railing against the government at the famous Speakers' Corner in Hyde Park did not get arrested.

We very much enjoyed this month together in London.

In the Poland of the late 1940s, devastated by the war, it was easy to find a job, Janina writes in her memoirs. On building sites, in factories, steel works, offices, institutions and headquarters, everywhere heads and hands were needed. Anything was possible; there were no limits. You began your studies in 1948 in Warsaw. What was the situation like at the university, three years after the war had ended?

I attended the Academy of Social and Political Sciences, whose faculty was a hotchpotch of quickly rounded-up teachers, most of them rather mediocre. There were no textbooks and only a meagre collection of other books. The courses all took place in the evening, because most of the students were working. I don't think that I learned a lot there. The only positive was that it was there that I met Janina. My real education began after the Bachelor's degree, at the second level, at the University of Warsaw, where I studied for my Master's. There, my teachers were researchers of the calibre of Stanisław Ossowski, Julian Hochfeld, Tadeusz Kotarbiński, Bronisław Baczko and Leszek Kołakoswki.

What was the subject of your doctoral dissertation?

The ideas of two German philosophers of the so-called Badische Schule of 'cultural science', Wilhelm Windelband and Heinrich Rickert, both inspired by Max Weber. Theirs was a neo-Kantian philosophy with an emphasis on values.

Janina writes that, as a regular officer, you were an 'enthusiastic theatre-goer'. Which plays featured on the stages of communist Warsaw at the time?

At that time, the theatre played an extremely important role in Poland. The theatres were among the first buildings that were restored after the almost complete destruction of Warsaw by the Germans. The arts received generous financial support from the intellectuals who were in power – the first and the last time that this was the case in Polish history. You could watch plays by Friedrich Dürrenmatt, Bertolt Brecht, Eugène Ionesco, Luigi Pirandello, all with magnificent actors and directors. Of the films, I should primarily mention those of Italian neo-realism, Luchino Visconti, Sandro de Santis, Roberto Rosselini, Michelangelo Antonioni, Federico Fellini, but also the works of young East German, Czech and Hungarian filmmakers. There was also Luis Buñuel, and there were the classic French filmmakers, such as Jean Renoir.

When you were a boy, what did you want to become when you grew up?

From early childhood, I was excited by physics and cosmology. I intended to dedicate my life to their study. If I had not been exposed with such intensity to the human potential for inhumanity, I probably would have become a physicist. But the experience of bombed-out streets full of refugees, of the desperate attempts to escape the advancing Nazi troops, of the misery of exile that was simultaneously a lifesaving miracle, turned me into a vagabond and awakened my interest in the manifold and diverse ways of human life. My interest in physics and astronomy, however, has never left me.

What did you read as a child?

In the beginning, the typical books that boys read: everything by James Fenimore Cooper, Jack London, Zane Grey, Karl May, Jules Verne, Robert Louis Stevenson, Alexandre Dumas and, of the Polish authors, Kornel Makuszyński. Later, all, or almost all, Polish classics, prose as well as poetry: Adam Mickiewicz, Bolesław Prus, Henryk Sienkiewicz, Stefan Żeromski, Eliza Orzeszkowa, Julius Słowacki and others. But, two or three years before we fled from Poznań, I bade farewell to children's literature. The books of Victor Hugo, Charles Dickens and Leo Tolstoy, to name only the most important authors, became my new diet.

Did your parents read to you when you were little?

My father read to me before I went to bed. No matter how tired he was when he came home from work at eight o'clock in the evening, he never went to bed without reading a chapter to me. He thus infected me with his respect and passion for the printed word. Limiting myself to only those authors whose books I can definitely recall him reading to me: Jules Verne, Christian Andersen, Selma Lagerlöf and Sven Hedin. Sven Hedin, the important Swedish explorer, is responsible for my preference for travelling in the north rather than the south.

Jewishness and Ambivalence
Adaptation: why were Jews attracted to communism?

You have always been markedly restrained when it comes to revealing details of your own life. Your readers know what and how you think, but not who you are or where you come from. Can you tell me something about your family history, your father, your mother?

My father, Maurycy Bauman, was born in 1890 in Słupca, a little market town that was part of Prussia at the time. He died in 1960 in the Givat Brener kibbutz in Israel. He was an autodidact. Apart from attending a cheder, a traditional Jewish religious school, he did not enjoy any formal education. His father, who ran a shop in the village and had seven children, could not, or would not, finance any further education. My father taught himself several languages. He was a passionate reader, and also wrote his own texts. After his death, he left behind a large number of manuscripts in Yiddish. Neither I nor anyone else in the kibbutz was able to read them. Unfortunately, my sister, Teofila, who had emigrated to Palestine in 1938 and lived in the same kibbutz, chucked all his papers and writing books in the recycling bin.

Were your father's parents religious?

My paternal grandfather was a practising Orthodox Jew, but he had no knowledge of or interest in theological or cultural subtleties. My father, by contrast, inhabited the world of the intellect, a life-long exile from everything practical. And the more he cultivated this side of himself, the less religiously orthodox he became. Once a year, on Yom Kippur, the Day of Atonement, he fasted and went to synagogue. Early on, he became a secular Zionist, and remained so all his life. Zionism was his religion, so to speak.

And your mother?

My mother, Zofia, was born in 1884 in Włocławek, which was a regional hub at the time. Until 1914, it was ruled by the Russians, and in 1917, when my parents married, it was captured and occupied by the Germans. My maternal grandfather owned a factory that produced building materials. Coming from a well-to-do family, she was able to enjoy further education. She was infected with a passion for culture, and she had ambitions. Those ambitions were frustrated during all those years she spent in the kitchen, where, as I mentioned before, she performed her culinary alchemy, which would have to do as an outlet for her creative aspirations. In fact, this would turn out to stand her in good stead during the period from 1939 until her death in 1954. In those years, unique cooking skills such as hers were sorely needed, first in the wartime canteens of the Soviet Union, and later in the simple restaurants of post-war Warsaw.

What were your father's and mother's lines of work?

When they married, Leon Cohn, my maternal grandfather, gave the young couple a small textile shop in Poznań. My father, who was uniquely unsuited to business – he was permanently ruminating on whatever he had just read – very soon went bankrupt. He was unemployed for some time, and he even attempted suicide. Then, he got a job as a bookkeeper for one of the large shops in Poznań. He remained a bookkeeper through the years we lived in the Soviet Union, as well as after we returned to Poland in 1946, and in the kibbutz in Israel, where he emigrated after my mother's death.

Your father emigrated during the political 'thaw' that began after Khrushchev, at the twentieth party conference of the CPSU [Communist Party of the Soviet Union], denounced Stalin's crimes, putting an end to the personality cult around the dictator. Jews in Poland, some of whom had held positions in the communist party and in the Ministry of Public Security, the infamous secret police, were hated more than ever. A new wave of anti-Semitism led the Polish party leader, Władysław Gomułka, to open the door to emigration to Israel for Polish Jews. Your father was already close to 70 at that point, and your mother had just died. But your father took the opportunity and applied for a passport. He received it in February 1957, and he emigrated. Had your mother also wanted to go to Palestine? Did she share the Zionism of your father, who wanted to die in the land of his forefathers?

In my parental home, the atmosphere was anything but Zionist. My mother felt and considered herself entirely Polish. The idea of giving in to my father's dreams of emigrating to Israel would never have occurred to her. He had to wait until she was dead. Then, he was on the first available ship. My sister, Teofila, who had emigrated long before him, had been a fickle and thoroughly apolitical teenager when she had moved to Palestine. While she was still in Poznań, she probably would have found it very difficult to tell you what Zionism is. That is a testament to our father's incredibly liberal attitude: he wanted us to be honest and to be happy, regardless of what we did with our lives. He did not intervene. My parents sent Teofila to Israel before the Nazi invasion; they did not want to risk their daughter's life. When, in 1938, a 20-year-old Palestinian man came to Poznań for an international trade fair, met my sister and fell in love with her, my parents seized the opportunity. Teofila left us as his wife. My father later went to her kibbutz, where he soon found his life-long dreams about Zionism belied by reality.

You fell out with your father, Janina writes, because he had gone to the Israeli Embassy in Warsaw to ask for advice on emigration. That was after Stalin, in December 1952, had launched an anti-Semitic 'cleansing campaign'. This 'contact with the West' on the part of your father was the reason you were summarily thrown out of the army in January 1953. You were declared persona non grata *and shunned by your old army comrades. You reconciled with your father, but you rarely had any contact with your sister, Teofila, who lived in Israel. Why not?*

After Teofila left Poznań in 1938, I had only very little contact with her. For roughly fifteen years, we had none at all, and for about twenty-five years we kept in touch only by way of the occasional letter. I met her children and grandchildren when I was in Israel, between 1968 and 1970, but to be honest I had only very limited opportunities to talk with them, both because of our diverging interests and because of the language barrier. When I left Israel, our contact broke off completely. Teofila died in 1999 at the Givat Brener kibbutz. She had a daughter, two sons of her own and a stepson from her second husband.

What kind of childhood did you have? Did you grow up among other Jewish children?

We were the only Jewish family in the Jeżyce part of Poznań, and I was the only Jewish pupil at its primary school. I first met Jewish boys of my own age in 1938, when I entered secondary school. There were four of us, just as many as were allowed to be admitted. The Berger secondary school was the only one that accepted Jewish pupils, on the basis of a *numerus clausus*. All the non-Jewish boys in my class were Boy Scouts. I remember that I envied them mightily. Boys from the 'school bench ghetto', as the four places allocated to us were called, were not allowed to join. But one of my new friends was an active member of Hashomer Hatzair, the youth group of the socialist branch of the Zionist movement. He introduced me to this group, which was a kind of Jewish Harcerze, the Polish version of the Baden-Powell movement. A few months later, the war broke out and I ended up in the Soviet Union. My conversion was an easy one: I simply dropped the 'Zionist' part that had been loosely and artificially attached to the 'socialist' part. The Soviet groups, such as the Komsomol, the communist youth organization, were not divided along ethnic lines.

Where does the name Bauman come from?

'Baumann', with two 'n's, is the German spelling. When we returned to Poland and the Germans had left, my father registered us as 'Bauman', with one 'n'. When and how exactly that happened, I do not know. I did not witness it, and I cannot prove it.

Your wife Janina was in the Warsaw Ghetto as a 14-year-old girl, and she experienced the horrors of the Nazi terror. Almost all of Janina's family were murdered. Did she not want to leave Poland? On 14 May 1948, the State of Israel was founded as a safe harbour for Jews from around the world.

Because of her terrible experiences in Nazi-occupied Poland, Janina was, when I met her, determined to emigrate to Israel. In the end, she agreed to remain in Poland. It didn't take much to persuade her, because she knew nothing about Zionism and her interest in it was accidental and pretty superficial.

You quarrelled over the subject, Janina writes, but then she herself felt strangely relieved that you decided to both stay in Poland.

She sensed that Poland was her homeland. The image she had of Israel was of the loving mother who ultimately turns out to be a callous and cruel stepmother.

Janina writes that you considered Zionism incompatible with communism, and the erection of a 'fortress' for the homeless, besieged and persecuted Jews the act of a new nationalism. When you returned home with the Polish Army, did you witness anything of the Holocaust?

One of the first things I saw when my artillery group reached Lublin was Majdanek, one of the most terrible extermination camps that the Nazis built in occupied Poland. There were still heaps of corpses everywhere; their removal had only just begun. But, unlike Janina, who only just escaped deportation to an extermination camp, I never had to live in this world of horror and inhumanity. I only read and heard about it, like – thank God – most people.

In your book Modernity and the Holocaust, *you defend the provocative thesis that the idea of exterminating human beings on an industrial scale is a product of modernity – not specifically of German nationalism. So would Auschwitz still be possible today? And if so, under what circumstances?*

The modern age is not a genocidal age. It has simply made possible modern ways of carrying out genocide, through innovations like factory technology and bureaucracy, but in particular through the modern idea of changing the world, even of turning it upside down – the idea that we no longer have to accept the thought that, as mediaeval Europeans believed, we are forbidden from meddling in God's creation, even if we don't like something about it. In the past, one simply had to endure things.

We can remake the world exactly as we wish.

This is exactly the reason the modern age was also an era of destruction. The striving for improvement and perfection necessitated the extermination of countless people whose adaptation to the desired perfect scheme of things was deemed unlikely. Destruction was the very essence of the new, and the annihilation of all imperfections the condition for achieving perfection. The projects of the Nazis and the communists were the most conspicuous examples of this phenomenon. Both sought to eradicate, once and for all, any unregulated, random or unruly elements of the *conditio humana.*

Was it the death of God that opened the door to this? Notwithstanding the fact that, in earlier ages, such as the time of the Crusades, murder was committed in the name of God.

The ambition of the modern age is to bring the world under our own management. Now, we are at the helm – not nature, not God. God created the world. But now that He is absent or dead, we manage it ourselves, make all things anew. The destruction of the European Jewry was only part of a larger project: the resettlement of all peoples, with the Germans at the centre – a monstrous undertaking, as dizzying as it was arrogant. One element that was essential for its execution is fortunately now absent: total power. This sort of project could only be carried out by communist Russia or Nazi Germany. In less totalitarian countries, like Italy under Mussolini or Spain under Franco, it wasn't possible. This element was lacking. May God help us that this will remain the case.

But the National Socialist project is often understood as just the opposite: as a return to barbarism, as a rebellion against modernity, against the core principles of modern civilization, and not as a continuation of modernity.

That's a misunderstanding. It stems from the fact that these were such extreme, infinitely radical manifestations of those core principles, and that those advancing them were ready to cast aside any scruples. National Socialists and communists were only doing what others also wanted to do at the time but weren't determined or ruthless enough to carry out – and what we still do today, albeit in a less spectacular and less repulsive fashion.

What do you mean?

The distancing of human beings from each other and the automation of human interaction, which we continue to pursue. All of today's technologies come down to this. Being able to avoid human contact wherever possible is considered progress. As a consequence, we can act without feeling any of the scruples that we inevitably have when we confront a person directly.

The Jews were the first to experience 'ambivalence', the conditio humana *of modernity. You also engaged with questions of ambiguity at a theoretical level.*

The Jews were the first to be exposed to ambivalence. They were involuntary discoverers of the new world – the avant-garde of ambivalence, if you like. Before anyone else, they entered into this state, which is characteristic of the liquid modernity in which we live.

To what extent are your thoughts about the concept of ambivalence based on your own experience of anti-Semitism in communist Poland? During the unrest of

March 1968, you lost your Chair and had to leave the country.

It helped, I think. It is very difficult to investigate the logic of one's own soul. That is always done retrospectively, with hindsight and with the knowledge acquired after the event – there is no other way. The question is whether, at the time that I started thinking about the issue of ambivalence, I was really aware of the motives that I see today when I look back. Was it part of my thinking at the time, or did I come across it later with the help of knowledge acquired afterwards? I can't tell.

Possibly both.

Logically speaking, you are right to assume that it had to do with my experiences in Poland. Like all assimilated Jews in Warsaw, I had a dramatic romance with 'Polishness'. I fell in love with Polish culture, the Polish language, Polish literature, everything Polish, but I was denied the right to belong to Poland, because I was a stranger. Tadeusz Kotarbiński, the well-known Polish philosopher and one of my teachers at university – who in his spare time wrote lyric poetry – said something fitting about this. I remember his poem on the subject well. The volume was titled *Cheerful Sadnesses.*

A paradoxical title – the ambivalence of a feeling!

Kotarbiński was a logician; he hated ambivalence. It disturbed him, and he fought against it. But he was very good at capturing ambivalence. It inspired him to write. The poem is about the socialist-leaning son of a large landowner. He's not a careerist. He's someone who really wants to be involved, wants to help build a better society. He asks one of the party members: 'What must I do for you to accept me?' And the answer is: 'You must stop being the son of a landowner.'

That is as impossible as stopping being a Jew.

I could not, and did not want to, stop being what I was: faithful to the Jewish tradition and, at the same time, the Polish tradition. I defined myself as a Pole, and I still so define myself today. You may have noticed that the reviewers of my books always refer to me as a Polish sociologist. But for a Jew to be referred to in that way, he has to leave Poland.

You have now lived in England for over forty years. What about Polish food? Do you eat borscht, bigos, duck with apples?

Not all that often, because we have to get the ingredients from Polish shops. They are not universally available. But, yes, of course I love Polish cuisine. Bigos and pirogi – Polish ravioli – I love in particular. And then there's something that is very popular in Poland but that you could not get in England until recently, until the wave of immigration from Poland set in: herring. That was not known here. But now you can buy herring. [*Bauman gestures to a bowl containing croissants and other pastries.*] But you haven't tried these products of French cuisine yet! Please, help yourself. They have been baked especially for you!

Many thanks!

And why do you not try these wonderful strawberries? There is no excuse for that!

You always serve up so much food that I don't know where to begin! And then I find it difficult to eat while concentrating on our conversation, especially given the seriousness of the topics. Where were we? Ah, yes: Karl Marx, the founder of so-called scientific socialism, was a Jew. Were you also disappointed about the way you were treated because you thought that socialism might have put

an end to ethnic pigeonholing and anti-Semitism? Did you
think a socialist society would be an egalitarian society in
which a person's ethnicity, race or language didn't matter?

Several authors have explained the relatively high number
of Jews in communist and socialist movements by saying
that membership in these groups allowed Jews to overcome
their ambivalence regarding their identity. The communist
party was not interested in the ethnic origin of potential
members but in conformity, loyalty and obedience. Ethnic
belonging was irrelevant. The very moment you joined the
party, you shed your ethnic origin like an old skin. At least,
that is how it seemed in the 1930s. But soon this turned
out to have been an illusion, and the idea of communism
developed into nationalist Bolshevism. Yet I do think that
the source of the attraction the communist movement held
for the Jews lay precisely there: communist organizations
were the only place where they could feel that they were
of equal value to anyone else. They no longer represented
an inferior minority.

And the communists were the fiercest enemies of the
Nazis, whose programme aimed at the 'annihilation of
the Jewish race in Europe', as Hitler had announced in his
Reichstag speech of 30 January 1939.[8]

Oh yes, that is an important point. The communist
movement was the only movement that was consistently
anti-Nazi. And I remember many people in the 1930s
– I was a child at the time – saying that the only choice
was that between Nazism and communism. Those were
the only options. The attitude of Western democracies
towards the Nazis was very lax. They treated them as
partners, as equal players in the political game. And the
Jews sensed what was coming. For them, it was a question
of life and death. But non-Jews who were concerned about
the future of the world also reached the conclusion that
the only genuine choice was that between Nazism and

communism. The others were simply silent witnesses of the catastrophe.

You were expelled from Poland because you were Jewish, and you lost your Polish citizenship. You went to Israel, but did not stay there for long. Zionism did not appeal to you, once you had familiarized yourself with it. Why not?

Oh my God. That is a very painful question.

I know.

It's true that I never felt attracted to Zionism. Why did I not want to stay in Israel? The reason for that is simple. I came to Israel because I had been thrown out of Poland. By whom? By Polish nationalists. And in Israel I was asked to become a nationalist, a Jewish nationalist. It is an absurd, alarming idea to seek to remedy nationalism with another nationalism. The only appropriate response to nationalism is to try to make it non-existent. While I was living in Israel, I published an article in *Haaretz*, Israel's liberal daily newspaper, setting out my observations. The title was roughly: 'It Is Israel's Duty to Prepare for Peace'. This article contains the only prediction I have ever made that turned out to be 100 per cent correct. It took some insight and some courage to predict, in 1971, what was going to happen to Israeli society, to the spirit of the Israelis, their consciousness, morality, ethics, etc. The West was still celebrating Israel's victory in the Six Day War: a small country had fought and won against large and powerful countries – David against Goliath. I wrote that there was no such thing as a humane occupation, and that the Israeli occupation of the Palestinian territories scarcely differed from other historical examples of occupation. They were all immoral, cruel and unscrupulous. It is not only the subjugated peoples who are harmed by occupation; the occupiers are harmed too. Occupation degrades them morally, and in the long term weakens them. I further predicted a militarization of the Israeli psyche and of Israel's ruling class, saying that the army would rule the nation, and not the nation the army. This is exactly what happened – to an extent that even I had not dared to predict. Today, about 80 per cent of Israeli citizens have only ever known war. War is their natural habitat. I suspect that the majority of Israelis do not want peace – in part because they have forgotten how to deal with the problems of social life during peacetime, during a time when problems can't be solved by dropping bombs and burning down houses. The people have never had the opportunity to learn how to pursue alternative solutions to difficult problems – solutions that do not involve the use of violence. Violence is in their blood. It is their way of viewing the world. Israel has manoeuvred itself into a cul-de-sac. I cannot even say that I am optimistic about the long-term prospects, even though, in other cases, I always am. For I really do not see a solution. I do not see a solution for the simple reason that I think in socio-logical terms. In order for there to be a solution, there must be someone, or a sufficiently strong group of people, to implement a plan. But in Israel the forces of peace are marginalized and insignificant. They wield no influence and no one listens to them.

Regarding the will for peace, the situation is not much different in the case of the Palestinians.

Yes, there is the same intransigence there, the same irreconcilability. The Palestinians have been frustrated so many times. They've seen how promises have been broken – how, over the years, Israel's demands have not weakened, so as to open up a space for negotiation, but on the contrary intensified. Whenever an urgent meeting between Israelis and Palestinians is coming up, the Israeli government announces the building of new settlements, taking away another part of Palestinian territory. I am really not an optimist in this case. I prefer not to think about it. In a sense, I'm even glad that I shall die soon and will not have to witness the likely tragic conclusion of the conflict. Have you read my book *Modernity and Ambivalence*?

It addresses the question of Zionism, among other things.

That book expresses my opinion on the matter. Zionism was, without a doubt, a product of European nationalism. Theodor Herzl, the founder of Zionism, had a slogan: 'A land without a people for a people without a land'. That is the slogan on which the whole era of European imperialism is based. The colonies were considered no man's land. The colonial masters ignored the fact that there were already people there. To them, these people were savages living in primitive conditions, in caves and forests, far away from civilization. They were poor and powerless, could be neglected and were not recognized as a problem. The same happened with Israel and Zionism. I think it is the last remnant of the imperialist era of European history. Well, maybe not the last – there are a few others – but certainly the most spectacular. And that is why Zionism is nothing but a variation of European imperialism. But I can understand Herzl. It was an idea of his time: we are a civilized people, and we shall bring civilization to this country of savages.

Intellect and Commitment

Sociology: why it should not separate objective from personal experience

Not only in Israel did you exercise your right to speak your mind. Jean-Paul Sartre considered it the task of the intellectual to criticize the ideology of the ruling class and to educate the people. Michel Foucault, by contrast, advocated the idea of the 'specific' intellectual: the expert in specific matters. The idea of the writer as representing the conscience of all, as a 'universal' intellectual, is opposed to the idea of the intellectual as political, committed and aiming at power. You were influenced by both thinkers. On this particular question, whose position are you inclined towards?

Michel Foucault observed that these 'specific intellectuals' have come to replace the earlier 'universal intellectuals'. A 'specific intellectual' knows his way around his discipline and is committed to it. Journalists fight for freedom of the press, surgeons for more resources for hospitals, actors for the funding of theatres: each for his own professional interest. I think that Foucault's concept of the 'universal intellectual', which he distinguishes from the new, 'specific' intellectual, is a tautology. 'Intellectual' means, by definition, something universal. Ever since the term was coined in the nineteenth century, an 'intellectual' has been understood as someone who keeps in mind the general interest of society, beyond his or her professional capacity and rank, someone who reflects on social values, morality and standards of living. Speaking of a 'universal intellectual' is like speaking of 'buttery butter' or 'metallic metal'.

Which means that 'specific intellectual' is a contradiction in terms.

The concept is an oxymoron, that's right. A 'specific intellectual' might be an educated person, but he is not an intellectual. Intellectuals exist to observe what is going on in society, a task that reaches far beyond someone's limited personal or professional interest. They are meant to serve the people of their country.

In current debates, however, intellectuals hardly figure at all. The populism raging in Europe and America has brought it about that facts hardly matter in political debate. What is important is not what is true but only what is believed.

On this point, I am even more sceptical than you are. Whoever seeks the truth does not enter politics at all. Politics is not about truth but about power. Whatever helps one achieve one's goals is good. There is no other form of politics.

But something like a discourse of reason used to exist in politics. Intellectuals worthy of the name should cultivate it.

Intellectuals exist in order to preserve values that transcend the changeable political scene. Politicians, in principle, should care about what is happening at the present moment. The task of the intellectual is more difficult. Intellectuals are meant to swim against the tide, to rescue the possibilities that were forfeited in the past. Those possibilities are not dead. They have simply been temporarily pushed aside – not been tested or put into practice. They must be preserved for future times. Intellectual work is a long-term activity; politics is short term.

It is important, though, that politicians look further than the next election. The problems are certainly longer term than that.

Imagine a politician who entered an election campaign with a fantastic programme for 2060. He would not stand the slightest chance. Instead, he rattles off slogans about the most recent terror attack, the latest corruption scandal, and he gets a lot of votes. If he shouts about yesterday's headlines, about the million Syrians knocking on Europe's door, he instantly has a large group of followers. People like Marine le Pen in France or Viktor Orbán in Hungary are masters of this strategy. They make huge political gains that way. But those who want to serve the truth, who have a long-term perspective? You would never expect such a person to become a politician.

Your body of work now includes almost sixty books. When do you write – at fixed times or spontaneously?

The morning is the creative part of my day. The day itself is divided into production and investment. From five in the morning until twelve o'clock, I am productive. That is what I can manage. Then I have lunch and take a short nap. The second part of the day is dedicated to investment.

Meaning, you read?

Yes.

You probably also have to respond to a lot of emails.

That's true, but most of them I delete without reading – lots of spam. I can't complain about a lack of interest in my work. In my life I have had plenty of opportunities to do things, more than the average person.

George Orwell, a writer you admire, asked himself a question that, actually, one should never ask an author. In his name, I take the liberty of putting it to you: why do you write?

George Orwell was a master juggler of words, and at the same time a very strict judge of the effects of this juggling. He was an exquisite aesthete, and his work provides a standard against which to judge any writing. Orwell says that, when he was 16, he suddenly discovered the 'joy of mere words', of 'the sound and association of words'. He had wanted to write, he says, in his essay 'Why I Write', 'enormous naturalistic novels with unhappy endings, full of detailed descriptions and arresting similes, and also full of purple passages in which words were used partly for the sake of their sound'.[9] I came to writing from the opposite pole. There were things I wanted to share with others, and the words were no more than servants of that purpose. Once committed to paper, I no longer cared about the words. My first article, which I sent to the youth supplement of the daily newspaper *Nasz Przegląd* when I was 11 years old, and which was actually printed, concerned the French linguist Jean-François Champollion. I had just read something about him and was deeply impressed by the fact that, after many failed attempts, he had succeeded in deciphering the Egyptian hieroglyphs, texts which for thousands of years had remained unread. I was so excited by it that I wanted to tell the story to the whole world. Orwell, by contrast, mentions 'aesthetic enthusiasm' as one of the four motivations for writing: the 'perception of beauty in the external world, or, on the other hand, in words and their right arrangement'.[10] I would be lying if I said that this was one of my motivations.

Your style, your feeling for language, your sense of rhythm and dramatic composition belie that.

After having several academic works published, I had the undeserved stroke of luck of being assigned Maria Ofierska, of the publishing house PWN (Polskie Wydawnictwo Naukowe), as my editor. She opened my eyes to 'the beauty of words' and their 'right arrangement'. It was not easy for her, as she had to deal with a pupil who was at first grumpy, then enthusiastic but slow-witted. Remembering her, I feel a mixture of deep remorse, bad conscience and enormous gratitude. She was heroic in the performance of her Herculean – and at the same time Sisyphean – task: drumming respect and a minimum level of appreciation for the powerful charm and charming power of words into a mind that had ideas to express but did not know, nor could feel, the right way to express them. All I know about the noble art of writing and the responsibility a writer has, not only for the correctness of the thoughts but also for the beauty of the language, I owe to her. I am still ashamed that I did not satisfy the high standards she set for me, that I was not able to reach that level. I am certainly not what the French call a 'littérateur', or the German a 'Dichter'. My craft is not that of *belles-lettres* – literature as an end in itself. But it would make me happy if I possessed the skill.

Can you go into more detail about your motivations?

Of paramount importance in my case are two of the four reasons Orwell lists in his answer to the question of why he writes: the 'historical impulse' and the 'political purpose', that is, on the one hand, the 'desire to see things as they are, to find out true facts and store them up for the use of posterity', and, on the other hand, the 'desire to push the

world in a certain direction, to alter other people's idea of
the kind of society that they should strive after'.[11] I think
this is where I would follow Orwell.

In terms of what motivates me, I can only paraphrase
Claude Lévi-Strauss's observation and say that I, too,
let the thoughts think themselves rather than motivating
them. And in this I have always been able to rely on the
world, as maddeningly fascinating, infuriating and mysterious as it is – now, and back then when I began to think
my first thoughts. You see, I have been alive for quite
some time, so there have always been new topics, new
problems, arising, that I have had to understand. There
is an inexhaustible supply of ideas in the world, which
militates against the temptation to rest.

*Your writing is very disciplined. It seems designed to draw
in the reader.*

To say that in hindsight would be wrong. It is impossible to impose discipline on spontaneity, or logic on the
unpredictable. My thoughts are conceived and delivered
by a world that is not exactly famous for its discipline
and logic. A book must be consistent, but the world does
not feel itself bound by any demand for consistency. It
does not have to be rigorous or conclusive. My method
of writing resembles the attempt to catch a mouse that's
running away by pouring salt on its tail: as Polish folk
wisdom will tell you, this is a method doomed to failure.
In my work, it is the rule rather than the exception that
the final full stop means 'to be continued' – that it represents a painful feeling of incompleteness. I try to heed
Michelangelo's advice to sculptors: that one needs only to
chisel away all the superfluous marble. So I embark on the
process of trimming as soon as I have written something.
I cut off the loose ends that threaten to distract the reader
from the main thread. Before the final full stop is set down,
I will have made quite a number of such cuts, each of them
a potential point of departure for a further book. When it

comes to the question of why I write, I can ultimately only repeat what I said in my little book *This Is Not a Diary*:

> I guess the question 'because of what' is more in order in this case than the question 'what for'. Causes to write are abundant, a crowd of volunteers line up to be noted, picked and chosen. The decision to start writing is, so to speak, 'overdetermined'. To begin with, I've failed to learn any other form of life except writing. A day without scribbling feels like a day wasted or criminally aborted, a duty neglected, a calling betrayed.[12]

You are not an ivory-tower academic. How important is it for you not to be writing just for an expert audience?

I am a voice in the wilderness, you know.

No, many people listen to you. Your books have been translated into many languages and are read by thousands and thousands, if not millions, all over the world.

Look, I have made a number of mistakes, mistaken judgements, mistakes in life. But there was one constant: I wanted to improve the world. And now I have one foot in the grave, and the world is no better. So my whole life's work has led nowhere.

Do you think the world has become worse or simply different?

That is a very important question that is difficult to answer. What I am concerned with is how to turn words into deeds. That is my obsession now. I am an old man, a man of a different time. I write, give lectures, travel around the world, but my fate is that of Norbert Elias, the author of *On the Process of Civilization*. He worked with Karl Mannheim, and was a personal student of Sigmund Freud. He wrote like Freud, in the same style he had learned as a student. And what is he today? A curiosity, a relic from a past epoch. I fear that I am coming to be perceived in the same way.

I do not think so. On the contrary, young people who do not accept that we are living in the best of all possible worlds quote your work: the opponents of globalization, members of the Occupy movement, whoever rejects the status quo of casino, turbo and finance capitalism.

I do not belong to the present times. Norbert Elias did not try to write about his own times. He stopped at the Second World War. But I am trying to understand and investigate a generation to which I do not belong. I want to know how the members of this generation feel, what they do. Whether I am going about this the right way is not for me to judge.

Your brand of sociology will have its followers, scholars who have been inspired by your way of thinking, your methods of exploring what many sense but cannot formulate.

There are a few people who find that useful. Others think what I do has nothing at all to do with sociology.

That's the ivory tower speaking: the scholars who want to keep to themselves because they cannot make themselves understood to others.

I don't care about how critics see me or what they call me. What is important to me is whether what I do speaks to someone, corresponds to his or her feelings and needs, or whether it is altogether useless. The boundaries between scientific fields are set by bureaucratic requirements. There is an administration; funds must be allocated, students assigned and doctorates handed out. One by-product of all this is the prevention of a merging of different fields.

This represents a particular loss in the case of sociology, the science of human life. People do not live within the confines of academic disciplines. They do not practise psychology in the morning, economy at midday, and politics late in the evening. From the perspective of human experience, these are artificial divisions.

So you are a Renaissance man, a universal scholar, interested in everything that is interesting.

No, that is not what I am, because there is one decisive difference. During the Renaissance, people had the advantage of still harbouring this vision of the world as a comprehensible whole. They still had the ability to process and make commonly understandable any information. When John Stuart Mill published his *Principles of Political Economy*, it was reviewed by the painter John Ruskin, the biologist Charles Darwin and the writer Charles Dickens. Today that would be inconceivable. A book on economics! Individuals from all sorts of professions and walks of life considered it their duty to respond because it was a cultural event, and they were all men of culture. That was the advantage of the Renaissance men. They lived before the rapid expansion of knowledge and its division into expert disciplines. We are a long way from this era. As you may know, the Sunday edition of the *New York Times* contains more information than a Renaissance man digested in the course of his life – a single Sunday edition.

But you have the curiosity of a Renaissance man.

As a young boy, I was convinced that we did not have sufficient knowledge to know what it was we should do. I believed that more studies, more books, more research were needed, and that then we would know what had to be done. Today, I believe the exact opposite. In drawing up a reasonable plan of action, the difficulty we face lies not in the lack, but in the overabundance, of information. We experience it daily. If you look to Google for an answer to a question, you will get millions of suggestions. How would it be possible to look at them all? An entire lifetime would not be long enough. We live in a world overflowing with information, and at the same time we are condemned permanently to feel insufficiently informed. That is the difference between the Renaissance and today. The internet, Facebook, LinkedIn, television, newspapers ... I cannot be a Renaissance man; no one can. It is too late. The Renaissance was different. They were lucky, the bastards!

So what can you be today?

You may hope that someone will find what you do useful. That there is a meaning in life. As far as I am concerned, I feel a mild despair. I produced a few good ideas, but they have not left any traces in the world.

With all due respect, I do not believe that you are in a position to judge this. There are trends in intellectual life, and, when it comes to the appreciation of your work, there are some positive signs. After the events of 1989, your compatriot Stanisław Lem had the very same feelings that you are describing. Despite being an author with a global reputation, no one in Poland was interested in him anymore. And then, following Poland's sobering experience with raw capitalism, everyone wanted to go on a pilgrimage to the wise man of Kraków. Are you familiar with his work?

Oh yes, I possess his collected works in Polish. Lem was a unique combination: a truly profound scientist and a very profound philosopher. That is rare. He was also a very good writer.

With a wonderful sense of humour.

Incomparable. The only person I could compare him to

would be Umberto Eco. He had a similar combination of talents.

Lem once said that, while Umberto Eco was able to draw on encyclopaedias of the Middle Ages for his novel The Name of the Rose, *he, Lem, had to write all the encyclopaedias for his futuristic novels himself. Of course, there was some mischief behind this remark: he said it in order to allude to his genius. He knew who he was.*

Umberto Eco did the same – regarding hyperreality, the right to falsification. He was fantastic, a walking encyclopaedia. Any short essay by him presents an intimidating amount of knowledge in an idiosyncratic combination.

As in your case.

No. Compared to people like Lem or Eco, I am very superficial. I have no high expectations. I would like to believe that what I wrote and thought had an effect.

You still do research, but you no longer teach. Do you miss it?

The students kept me on my toes. They were eager to learn, contradicted me and spurred me on. They would ask a question; I would offer an explanation, and they were satisfied. But while I was giving the explanation, I would recognize that I had not understood the issue myself. Interaction with students was an essential part of my work. Without it, I would not have been able to formulate something clearly, to articulate a problem. Now, I no longer have regular students, but I am still being challenged and finding myself in situations where I can see the limits of my understanding. Aleksandra, my second wife, is very critical, and that helps. She is a professor at the University of Warsaw, a very good sociologist. She replaces a legion of students.

You used to travel a lot, and you still travel today. You have contacts all around the world, in Russia, China, Germany, France. Is travelling important to you?

My frequent travels may have something to do with the way my thoughts think themselves – that is, in the course of conversation. Since I no longer have any regular students to urge me on, I give guest lectures, which allow me to learn, receive explicit or tacit feedback and see whether my half-baked ideas taste good. This way, I find out what additional ingredients are needed to make the product palatable, so I can complete the baking process. After my lecturing jaunts, I usually return better prepared for future work. But I reject many invitations on account of the protest of my ageing body.

And what about travels in order to see the sights, to experience something?

I don't have a touristic bone in my body. I have no interest in going anywhere just to satisfy my curiosity – especially seeing that I can visit almost every art gallery on the planet on the internet, without having to spend valuable time in the nowhere space of the airport.

Power and Identity

Modernity: on the compulsion to be no one, or become someone else

Among the authors who had a formative influence on you are two who do not belong to your field of expertise, sociology: the writer Franz Kafka and the psychologist Sigmund Freud. What can they tell us about the conditio humana *today – about our life?*

That is not an easy question to answer. How can you put your finger on what they have to teach us today? The thought of the present is a communal product of authors like them. Once an idea is universally accepted, it is dead, because no one remembers where it came from. It then belongs to the class of truisms. Kafka was absolutely revolutionary; Freud was absolutely revolutionary. When we think about them today, they are orthodox. Ideas begin their lives as heresy, continue into orthodoxy and end as superstition. That is the fate of every thought in history. Kafka's and Freud's ideas are united in that they have become 'doxa', in the ancient Greek sense. They are generally held opinion.

Well, what was revolutionary about Kafka then?

His analyses of power and guilt. *The Trial* and *The Castle* are two foundational documents of modernity. In my opinion, no one has improved upon Kafka's analyses of power. Take *The Trial*. Someone is accused. He wants to know why he is accused, but he is unable to find out. He wants to provide a justification, but he does not know what it should be for. He is full of good will and determined to visit any institution that might provide him with clues. He tries in vain to gain access to the court. Finally, he is executed without ever having known what made him guilty. His guilt consists in having been accused.

The fundamental principle of criminal proceedings in a state under the rule of law is the presumption of innocence: the accused is innocent until proven guilty.

Kafka shows that it is the other way around. Because innocent individuals are not accused, whoever is accused must be guilty. Because he is taken to be guilty, Josef K., the protagonist, becomes a criminal. He must prove his own innocence. But in order to do so, he would need to know what he is being accused of. And he does not know that, and no one tells him. It is a tragic situation.

And in The Castle?

The novel's hero, K., assumes that certain people high up in the castle must be rational beings, although he does not know them, nor they him. It is all mysterious, impenetrable and inaccessible. K. fights in vain for the acknowledgement of his professional and private existence. But he continues to believe that the officials in the castle will behave rationally and that he can talk with them about the reasons for his defeat. Kafka tells us very little about K., but from the text we understand that he is probably an educated person. He is a rational man – someone who, as

Max Weber would say, chooses the appropriate means for his ends and assumes that others are rational, too. But this is not the case, and that is the massive mistake he makes – because the power of the inhabitants of the castle consists precisely in the fact that they behave irrationally. If they behaved rationally, it would be possible to negotiate with them, maybe to convince them or to fight against them and win. But if they are irrational beings, if their power is based on their irrationality, this is impossible.

The land surveyor K. cannot even get near the castle: the path is not where it should be; the telephone line does not work. The masters in the castle are like God, the Almighty, whose judgements are unsearchable, as the Bible says.[13]

In what I consider his most important work, *Political Theology*, Carl Schmitt, the political philosopher and Nazi crown jurist, reflected on what it means to be a sovereign. His idea was a bold one: the sovereign is a secular God. Like God, he makes decisions that he needs neither to explain nor to justify. He does not owe anything to anyone. He does not argue; he decides. I can't prove it, but I think that Carl Schmitt drew his inspiration from Kafka. Kafka had said something similar, albeit in fewer words.[14]

Theodor W. Adorno saw Kafka as a visionary who, in The Castle *and* The Trial, *anticipated in literary form the terror of the Nazis and the hierarchy and power structures of totalitarianism in general.*

Have you read the Bible?

Large parts of it.

Many people have not. Do you remember the Book of Job? In the Book of Job, in one of His rare conversations with a human being, God says very clearly: 'I ask the questions, and you are there to answer them.' God refuses to give any explanation for what He does. To be God means not to owe any explanations to human beings.

It still remains somewhat odd that, of all people, a Catholic like Schmitt would deify dictators like Mussolini and Hitler.

Today, Carl Schmitt is a favourite author among the intellectual elite and has been rescued from the ignominy of being known as an abhorrent Nazi. There was a time when he was shamed, disgraced, a time when his past was not forgotten. But today his fame has been restored.

Why is Sigmund Freud important to you?

Like Kafka, Freud has become part of our thinking – common property, so to speak. We are familiar with concepts like the unconscious, with 'Id', 'Ego' and 'Super-Ego'. The American philosopher, sociologist and psychologist George Herbert Mead, who made a substantial contribution to our thinking about identity, does not use these terms, but he ultimately has the same thing in mind when he talks of 'I' and 'Me'. 'I' am what results from my thinking, what I really am, what is authentic. But I am divided because, in addition to this internal 'I', there is the external 'Me': namely what people around me think about me, how people view me, what people believe about how I really am. Our lives are a fight for a peaceful co-existence between the 'I' and the 'Me'. That is another way of telling the same story that Freud told.

Mead says an individual's identity is determined through interactions with other individuals. There are several different 'Me's, and the task of the 'I' is to synthesize them into a coherent self-image. Identity in its present form, in 'liquid' or 'fleeting' modernity, has something to do with this interplay, but it is much more complex. Nowadays, everyone has not only several 'Me's but also several

'I's. You have been concerned with this phenomenon in particular.

Today, identity is a question of negotiation. It is indeed liquid. We are not born with an identity that is given, once and for all, and will not change. What's more, we can have multiple identities simultaneously. In a conversation on Facebook, you may choose a certain identity, and in the next conversation you may choose another. You can change your identity at any time, and different identities go in and out of fashion. This interplay between 'I' and 'Super-Ego', or 'I' and 'Me', is part of our daily work. Freud prepared the ground for our understanding of this interplay.

The idea of identity as a kind of fashion accessory is something you discuss in the context of your critique of today's rampant consumerism. The consumer society, you say, makes it difficult to be happy because it depends on us being unhappy.

'Unhappy' is too grand a word in this context. But any marketing manager would insist that his products satisfy consumers. If that were true, we would not have a consumer economy. If needs were genuinely satisfied, there would be no reason to replace one product with the next.

The left of 1968 called this the 'terror of consumerism'. What is the difference between consumption and consumerism?

Consumption is a trait of individual people, and consumerism a characteristic of society. In consumerist societies, the capacity to want, wish and long for something is dissociated from the individual. It is reified, meaning it becomes a force outside the individual. It is difficult, almost impossible, to resist this force because everyone is subject to it. The desire to satisfy all commercially created needs becomes an addiction that takes hold of society as a whole.

What does this mean in concrete terms?

If we want to understand this, we need to take a look at history. At the end of the nineteenth century, many craftsmen lost their workshops and fell into poverty. But the new factory owners, whose actions had led to this development, found it difficult to find enough workers. As long as they had their daily bread, people were not prepared to submit themselves to the discipline required by the factory. The pioneers of the modern market economy dreaded the traditional craftsmen. The bogeyman of today's consumer economy is the traditional consumer, the person who is satisfied with the products she buys. In contrast to earlier forms of consumption, consumerism connects happiness not exactly to the satisfaction of needs, but to the growth of the number of desires. That growth requires a quick succession of objects to fulfil these desires. Although the consumerist society declares the satisfaction of the customer as its goal, a satisfied customer is in fact its greatest threat, because it only continues to flourish as long as its members are dissatisfied. The main goal of marketing is not to create new commodities but to create new needs. That is why products which only a moment ago were the *dernier cri*, and depicted as objects of desire by advertising, are suddenly ridiculed as being so 'yesterday'. Children as young as 5 are being trained to become insatiable consumers. On Sunday, they go shopping with their parents, in a world full of interesting, exciting and seductive commodities. Things are bought and kept until one grows tired of them and throws them away.

The market includes not just commodities but also consumers. As you say, they too are becoming commodities, which brings us back to the question of identity.

The culture of consumerism is characterized by a pressure to be someone else, to acquire characteristics for which there is a demand on the market. Today, you have to concern yourself with marketing, to conceive of yourself as a commodity, a product that can attract a clientele. Fully fledged members of consumerist society are consumer goods themselves. Paradoxically, however, this compulsion to imitate whatever lifestyle is currently being touted as desirable by marketeers, and thus to revise one's own identity, is not perceived as an outside pressure but as a manifestation of personal freedom.

Many teenagers today do not have concrete ideas about what they might do for a career other than an aim of becoming famous, with the help of posts on YouTube or by whatever other means. What does this mean?

To them, being famous means appearing on the front pages of thousands of papers or on millions of screens, being an object of conversation, being perceived and in demand – just like the bags, shoes and gadgets in the glossy magazines which they, in turn, desire. Transforming oneself into a desirable, marketable commodity improves one's chances in the competition for the lion's share of attention, fame and wealth. That is the stuff today's dreams and fairy-tales are made of.

According to the French sociologist François de Singly, identity is no longer a matter of roots. Instead, he uses the metaphor of the anchor. Unlike uprooting oneself, liberating oneself from social tutelage, there is nothing irreversible or final about the raising of an anchor. What do you dislike about this?

We can only become someone else if we stop being who we are now, so we perpetually have to discard our previous selves. Because of the constant stream of new options, we soon come to see our current self as outmoded, unsatisfying and constraining.

Isn't there something liberating about the ability to transform who we are? In America, in the New World, that was and still is the mantra: re-invent yourself!

Of course, this is not a new strategy: to turn tail and run away when the going gets tough. People have always tried it. What is new, however, is the desire to flee from ourselves by picking a new self from a catalogue. What might start out as a self-confident step towards a new horizon quickly turns into an obsessive routine. The liberating 'you can become someone else' becomes the compulsive 'you must become someone else'. This 'must-do' sense of obligation hardly resembles the freedom people are seeking, and many people rebel against it for this very reason.

What does it mean to be free?

Being free means being able to pursue one's own desires and goals. The consumption-oriented art of living in the age of liquid modernity promises this freedom, but fails to deliver on its promise.

This brings us back to Sigmund Freud, who addressed the relationship between freedom and security in his Civilization and Its Discontents. *He wrote of the opposition between civilization and instinct. It is impossible to achieve fulfilment in one without giving up on the other: civilization is the renunciation of instinctual gratification.*

Freud is a daily inspiration for me on so many questions. He defined civilization as a deal, an exchange of values. There are two values that are important to you. You want to pursue both, but unfortunately you can't. The more you achieve one of them, the less you get of the other. In 1929, Freud wrote that the major psychological afflictions of the age arise because we have sacrificed a large amount of personal freedom in order to enjoy the increased security provided by civilization – security against all sorts of dangers: natural forces, previously incurable illnesses, violent neighbours who run around armed with knives and, of course, our own morbid instincts. Our behaviour becomes civilized. We develop the capacity to resist the false guidance of instinct, as the Canadian sociologist Erving Goffman put it. We do not attack people simply because we take a dislike to them. We do not succumb to our desire for revenge. We display a civilized indifference, a kind of attitude that signals that we are not aggressive but tolerant, which involves simply not paying attention to someone. To exhibit indifference is also an achievement of civilization.

Goffman speaks of 'civil inattention'. For Richard Sennett, civility means 'the shielding of others from being burdened with oneself'.[15] That virtue, however, has been jettisoned in the age of the selfie. You do not fear, as Freud did, that we lack freedom – especially as the satisfaction of sexual desire is far less restricted today than it was in fin-de-siècle *Vienna.*

If Sigmund Freud were sitting here today instead of me, he would still probably say that civilization is an exchange, but I think he would turn his diagnosis upside down. He would say that the psychological afflictions of the present result from the fact that we have forfeited too much of our security in favour of an unprotected realm of freedom. That is what I am interested in. I could not imagine my work without this Freudian inspiration. At best, all I am doing is revising his discoveries in light of developments.

What is the security, then, which we have sacrificed for the freedoms we enjoy?

We are now responsible for finding solutions to problems we did not create. I always return to the late sociologist Ulrich Beck on this point: today's individuals, he says, must use their own talents and ingenuity to find individual solutions for social problems. In contrast to previous times, these problems are no longer produced locally in Paris, Berlin or Warsaw, but globally. There is nowhere to turn. We live in a 'space of flows', as the Spanish sociologist Manuel Castells puts it. Everything is in flow. The problems are moving, caused extraterritorially, and they are not contained by local rules and laws. An entrepreneur who feels restricted can at any point move somewhere else or shift his capital to another place.

That is less true for employees; they are less mobile. That is the reason for the protests against globalization.

In most countries, we therefore see calls for strong government. The people have had enough of being free without limitation, because such freedom has risks attached to it. There is no freedom without risk. Because of the extent to which society is privatized and individualized, we are all individuals by decree. We cannot shed the duties of the individual; they are commanded of us. On the one hand, that is a blessing. We are able to serve ourselves, to determine for ourselves who we are to be. But, on the other, we are continually frustrated. We constantly feel that we are insufficient. This loss makes the individual an orphan.

What was it like when you were young?

When I was young, the nightmare scenario was being a non-conformist. The aim was not to deviate. Today, the nightmare scenario is not being up to the scale of the task. Across Europe, people are tired, and new political movements, apparently springing up from nowhere, are making grand promises. Something similar happened in the seventies, when people had dreams that a strongman would come along and solve all the problems that were proving so intractable. Candidates aspiring to that role offered a simple programme: 'Trust me, give me power and I will do whatever needs doing.' This kind of politician declares himself omniscient and almighty – as with Donald Trump in the US today.

It is the cry for a father who puts everything right, who takes you by the hand and leads you safely through the dark forest.

Let me tell you two fictional anecdotes on this theme. The first is from Aleksandr Solzhenitsyn's novel *Cancer Ward*. There is an interesting character in that book – a communist dignitary who lives on the cancer ward waiting for a difficult operation that may well kill him. But he is happy. He is the only person on the ward who never complains. Every morning, he receives the latest edition of *Pravda*, the communist party paper. He reads it, and then he learns which names he can mention, which names he must not mention and what the topics of the day are. He does not have responsibility for anything; he is safe and does not worry. The other example is from the Soviet film *The Vow*, made by Mikheil Chiaureli, an excellent director from Georgia: an important film in a cinematographic sense but, politically, utterly toxic. In this film, there is a nameless Russian mother – a wonderful woman, loving and lovable – who goes to Stalin and tells him: 'Look, we have been at war now for several years. People are exhausted. So many of us have lost husbands, children, fathers. Comrade Stalin, it is time to end the war.' And Stalin says: 'Yes, mother, you are right. It is time to end the war.' And he ends the war. No sociologist would be capable of describing the mechanism of power, the omnipotence of a dictator, as perspicuously as this.

The Lord gave, and the Lord hath taken away; blessed be the name of the Lord. Stalin is the God of the Book of Job.[16]

Why was the war continuing? Because Stalin thought that it was not yet time to end it. The women wish that he should end it, and he ends it. That is the essence of omnipotence, the longing for a strong leader. Those who long for such a leader get frustrated with democracy, not because democracy means freedom – that is nonsense – but because democracy does not keep the promises it makes. Political parties make promises, get into power, and cannot fulfil their promises. This is not because they are corrupt but because they are not in a position to do so.

You engaged deeply with the work of philosophical sociologist Georg Simmel, an outsider to his discipline who was, in a certain sense, your teacher. Like you, he made use of material from other fields, from anthropology to psychology. His influence, like yours, reached far beyond his discipline.

Georg Simmel is the sociologist's sociologist. Unlike Freud or Kafka, he did not write for the broader educated masses. He fought for the kind of sociology he thought we should be doing. I learned the art of sociology from him. My own sociological style is an imitation, a pale imitation, of his sociology, of the way he approached problems.

In 1909, Simmel founded the Deutsche Gesellschaft für Soziologie, together with Ferdinand Tönnies, Max Weber and Werner Sombart. Some people criticized Simmel for being an eclectic.

Max Weber criticized Simmel for not distinguishing between the actual situation and the human perception of the situation – in his eyes a grave mistake, almost a crime. My opinion on this is decidedly different from Weber's, because I consider this characteristic of Simmel his greatest strength. He was interested in the dialectic between perception and reality.

The Kantian revolution made this idea part of our common

intellectual heritage, but to make it fruitful for sociology was novel.

Simmel was absolutely revolutionary. In German, there are two nouns which are translated into English as one and the same noun – namely, as 'experience'. German has two words, 'Erfahrung' and 'Erlebnis', for 'experience'. They are both aspects of 'experience', but they differ greatly. 'Erfahrung' is what happens to me. 'Erlebnis' what happens inside of me – what I feel, sense, the emotional results of events. My whole sociology moves in the space between 'Erfahrung' and 'Erlebnis'. It is difficult for me to explain this to an English-speaking audience because English only has the one word for it. Germans understand what I mean on the basis of just one sentence. For an English-language audience, I need a whole page to explain it.

Apart from Kafka, Freud and Simmel, which other authors had a big influence on you?

There are several who have played a role in my thinking, each with a style and substance of their own. I have already mentioned Antonio Gramsci. I can't stress enough how much I owe to him. He allowed me to achieve an honourable departure from Marxism: only through him was I able to stop being an orthodox Marxist without becoming an anti-Marxist. My friend Leszek Kołakowski could not do that. He could break with Marxism only by becoming an anti-Marxist. He probably did not read Gramsci; I don't know. Antonio Gramsci is one of the most humorous, most humane philosophers that I know of.

And modern thinkers?

Claude Lévi-Strauss, who is considered the founder of ethnological structuralism, is particularly important to me. There was a time in my life, in the late sixties, when I was completely enchanted by Lévi-Strauss. What did I take from him? Well, I am very eclectic: wherever I find something exciting that fits into my thinking, I use it. But I do not feel obliged to accept a thinker wholesale. What I took from Lévi-Strauss was the idea of getting away from the image of a culture as a body. Instead of reflecting on differences between cultures, he spoke of universal methods. He spoke not of 'culture' but of 'structure', and he went down in history as a structuralist. But, in fact, he gave up the idea of a structure, a given organization, an arrangement of things. He insisted on the universality of structuring. Structure, for him, was an activity: not a body but a kind of uncertain, never-ending activity. Nothing is done once and for all; structures are not ossified, petrified, immutable. And that is precisely how I try to describe reality, social realities and dynamics of social realities. At the centre of my research is culture as a dynamic process that is never complete.

That is also how Gramsci saw it. That is something he shares with Lévi-Strauss.

Well, to Kafka, Freud and Simmel, I would add Antonio Gramsci and Claude Lévi-Strauss. But there is a whole range of non-academics, non-scientists, to whom I owe a lot – writers, novelists, most of all. Milan Kundera says the novel is the most important achievement of modern civilization. The invention of the novel comes about through the unification of biography and history. Biography and history are partly autonomous because each of them is ruled by its own logical pattern, but at the same time the one cannot exist without the other. Sociology must not neglect either of them. If – God forbid – one does, one gets either a sociology of 'Erfahrung' or a psychology of 'Erlebnis'. The whole point of sociology is to unite the two in order to demonstrate their interaction and dynamic.

You are politically active, if not in the narrow sense of the word. As a social scientist, you are not content with providing an analysis of society. You want to show that there are alternatives. That, for you, is the very point of sociology.

You are right about that. You see, I have lived for an inexcusably long time. That means that I have experienced a number of different trends in sociology. When I started out in sociology, the American sociologist Talcott Parsons was the dictator who determined what sociology was all about. His most important achievement was to introduce an idea of a kind of liberal-conservative utopia. Parsons saw the role of the sociologist as one of serving managers, helping them to solve their problems and to do their work better. How do you keep workers from going on strike? How do you avoid soldiers deserting, guerrillas committing terrorist attacks? And so on. We sociologists, he thought, should bring the system back into equilibrium by eliminating the troublemakers.

That is sociology in the service of the ruling class.

In the nineties, Michael Burawoy, an exceptionally brilliant British sociologist, sounded the alarm by stating that sociology was losing touch with the public sphere, losing the kind of relationship which French philosophers had with their public. What had taken place in the meantime was the individualization and privatization of social problems. This process led ultimately to what the British sociologist Anthony Giddens called 'life politics'. 'Life politics' is what happens when you or I, or any other individual, becomes the parliament, the government and the supreme court all in one: we must each solve all problems we confront ourselves, with our own resources and our own inventiveness, even if we were not responsible for creating them.

Society and Responsibility

Solidarity: why everyone becomes everyone else's enemy

From your first book on the British labour movement to your engagement with questions about postmodern ethics, your focus has shifted from social classes to the individual. It seems that what counts in the end is less the place someone occupies within society, and more what he does independently of it.

This is not simply a change in perspective from class to the individual. I reached the conclusion that, today, classes are statistical products and not the products of real life. On the basis of statistics, you may postulate as many classes as you like. You can categorize people according to their income, education, lifestyle, the respect and prestige they enjoy in society – according to any conceivable criterion. But these do not reflect the reality of life; they are ways of arranging things. This change is something we ourselves bring about through the processes of privatization and individualization. Functions which were once, a long time ago, social functions have become individual ones. For Max Weber – who, like almost everyone else at that time, accepted the idea that society was divided up into classes

– a class, by contrast, was defined in terms of objective similarities between living conditions. People belong to the same class when they are in the same boat.

Karl Marx, the originator of the concept of class, spoke of the 'class in itself' and the 'class for itself', in Hegel's sense. Becoming a 'class for itself' means developing a class consciousness.

In order to raise itself up from a 'class in itself' to a 'class for itself', a class must become politically active. It has to understand that all its members are in the same boat and have a shared destiny. It must fight to improve its situation. Today, this is often not happening. The trade unions have lost power, and the means for strengthening their negotiating positions, such as strikes, are no longer available.

What are the consequences of these changes?

The decline of the trade unions has made collective self-defence far more difficult. With the dismantling of the welfare state, which protected people against the blows of fate and individual failure, the social foundation of solidarity has been further eroded. It is now down to the individual to find solutions for problems that he did not cause. The individual is entirely on his own, and he lacks the tools and resources necessary to solve these problems. How can you express solidarity if you are constantly having to change jobs?

How did we get to this point?

Fifty, sixty years ago, the classic model of the relationship between capital and labour was the Ford factory. And the most important characteristic of the Ford factory was the mutual dependence between the factory owner and the workers. Workers in Detroit, the capital of the automotive industry, were dependent on Henry Ford. They earned their living in Ford's Dearborn factory, and without Ford they were without means. But Ford was just as dependent on them. The factory could not run without the workers. They made him rich, made him powerful. Even if neither side talked about it, articulated their feelings, they knew exactly that they were condemned to a life together – a very long life. They knew they were going to see each other again tomorrow, the next month, the next twenty years. When a young man started as an apprentice with Fiat or Peugeot, he could be certain that he would retire from the same company in forty or fifty years' time, perhaps with a golden watch to thank him for his decades of faithful service.

Workers or employees can no longer expect that today.

Everyone must reckon with the possibility that a large company will swallow up their small company, or that their bosses will, for whatever reason, move their capital to another country, somewhere where the workers are happy to accept 2 dollars a day and never go on strike. The unwritten contract between capitalist and labourer has been broken – on one side. The bosses can go wherever they like and do what they want, while the labourers and employees are still tied to a location. They are 'adscripti glebae', as serfs were called in the Middle Ages: tied to the land.

But there are also workers who emigrate, 'economic refugees'.

Yes, indeed, they can emigrate, but at what price? They have to pay exorbitant sums to people traffickers, embark on a risky journey across the Mediterranean; they then get stopped at the border, put in camps or sent home again. The poor seeking jobs, money and better schools for their children are still dependent on the bosses who purchase their labour, but the bosses are no longer dependent on them. They go wherever is most profitable for them. The effects of this are clear: the only workers who still occasionally go on strike are those employed by the state, with safe workplaces and contracts for life. Their jobs are practically non-terminable. But labour markets in some far-flung countries are completely unregulated. No one can risk going on strike, because the bosses will not come to the negotiating table to find a consensual solution.

Which means that the only people who can express solidarity are the ones who have no real need for it.

The proletariat is no longer a 'class for itself', as in Marx's times, because now everyone is responsible for him- or herself. Instead of solidarity and a sense of community developing among the workforce, there is the opposite. Every other worker is a potential competitor. Everyone is suspicious of everyone else. Each worker hopes that, when the next round of rationalization, downsizing and outsourcing comes along, someone else will be the victim, will become superfluous, and he himself will keep his job. This is what is in the interest of today's factory worker; he has nothing to gain by joining forces with others. Thus, everyone else becomes a potential enemy, and the chances that this class will raise itself from 'in itself' to 'for itself' are slim. During the time of solid modernity, by contrast, a Fordist factory, whatever goods it might have produced, also produced solidarity – a forced solidarity that had its basis in the logic of the situation. Today's factory, whatever goods it produces, also produces this rivalry.

Even formerly secure middle-class employees now fear this decline into a mass of lone wolves, worrying about losing their jobs from one day to the next.

It is no longer controversial to say that inequality is on the rise. Economists from a variety of different schools, applying various criteria, yield strikingly similar results on this. Since the beginning of the new millennium, the proceeds of economic growth have flowed almost exclusively into the pockets of the richest 1 per cent of the population – if not less than 1 per cent – while the income and wealth of the other 99 per cent have decreased, or threatened to decrease. In the so-called developed countries of the North, we have a situation that has not existed since the 1920s. The middle class is now part of the precariat. Even if a member of the middle class may be faring well enough, she has no firm ground to stand on. Members of the precariat live with the permanent nightmare of waking up the next day to find that their job no longer exists. Without any advance warning, one's position may be gone from one day to the next. I shifted my focus from class to the individual not because I have changed my views but because the situation has changed.

Even if class struggle is a thing of the past, political commitment, taking a stand for or against something, has not diminished – quite the contrary.

People commit themselves to all sorts of causes – environmental, ethical, religious. There has been a resurgence of interest in local issues. The fights are for state subsidies for particular causes, and in those fights people are in competition with one another. There are all kinds of conflicts and antagonisms, but none of them can be grasped in terms of class. The only battle reminiscent of class struggle is that between rich and poor. That is the topic of my new book *Retrotopia*: the 'two nations' of which Benjamin Disraeli, the conservative British statesman and writer, spoke in his 1845 novel *Sybil, or the Two Nations*. Disraeli's novel features a radical worker, Walter Gerard, who speaks of the country's 'two nations',

between whom there is no intercourse and no sympathy; who are as ignorant of each other's habits, thoughts, and feelings, as if they were dwellers in different zones, or inhabitants of different planets; who are formed by a different breeding, are fed by a different food, are ordered by different manners, and are not governed by the same laws.[17]

In other words, as another character, Charles Egremont, comments: the rich and the poor. This is a fitting image for the situation we find ourselves in today, 170 years later. But rich and poor are not classes, despite the fact that the battle between them can be expressed in social terms; nor, contrary to a widespread opinion, are revolutions carried out by people who live in poverty. The poor would be the rank and file, and the idea of uniting them under one banner, a class-based banner, comes from the intelligentsia, from educated people who have time to think. But today there is neither an intelligentsia offering something like this idea, nor candidates to serve as the rank and file who would be prepared to accept the offer. That is my answer to your question about the shift of focus. I think social reality has been transformed.

It was not so long ago that the fight against poverty, at least in Western industrial countries, looked as if it had almost been won.

Since Disraeli's analysis, efforts have been made to end poverty, and in the decades following the war there was a belief that the 'division into two nations' would soon be eliminated. Decent wages for work – that was the way out of poverty. And it was seen as the task of the government to use public spending to guarantee full employment, because the economy by itself would not deliver anything like it. People were convinced that the 'war against poverty needs to be waged and conducted by political organs deploying political weapons'.[18]

Today this would be difficult, especially because, as you

say, power and politics have come apart. How did this happen, and what does it mean?

When I was a student, more than half a century ago, the nation state was still the supreme institution. Within its territory, it was in every respect the sovereign – economically, militarily and culturally. That is no longer the case. Power has migrated out of politics: firstly into the global space, where multinational corporations rule; secondly into consumer markets that cannot be democratically directed and controlled; and thirdly to the citizens, who have to solve social problems with private means instead of the traditional political means – 'life politics', as it is called.

While the truly powerful – banks and corporations – operate globally, the influence of politicians remains local. How do we control power if we lack the means to do so?

Bringing politics and power back together is the greatest challenge of this century. Problems that are caused or aggravated by globalization can't be solved at the local level. That can only be done at the global level. To do this, politics would have to become sufficiently powerful.

But it does not have that power, as you keep repeating.

Politics is impotent. The decisions taken by politicians, by the people of Zurich, Budapest or Stockholm, are only valid within their local areas of authority. These are, in effect, the same local communities as we had 400 years ago. Power is globalized, but politics is as local as it has ever been. The people deciding your future, and that of your children, do not even live in the same country as you. The powers exerting the greatest influence on human living conditions and on the prospects for the future operate globally. They operate in what I referred to earlier as the 'space of flows'; they wilfully ignore borders, laws and the interests of political entities. Politics, by contrast, remains within the 'space of places'. As politics continues to lose power, these powers continue to emancipate themselves from political limitations and controls. No one can touch them. And nothing will change about that in the near future. We are caught in this situation in which we need all our private resources in order to deal with problems that are not of our own making. We are a society of individuals who must make their own decisions and take responsibility for the consequences.

Was it simpler in earlier times?

I grew up during a period of European history in which people were divided up into political camps: left and right, liberals and conservatives, communists and Nazis. But on one point they were all agreed: they knew that there was a state that had power, practised politics and had the tools and resources necessary to take effective action. The only problem was thus how to seize the power of the state in order to push through the changes you wanted to see. The people who suffered the consequences of the global economic crisis of the twenties and thirties had a plan. Rightly or wrongly, they believed that a strong state – whether a National Socialist or a communist one – would be able to solve the problems. The people who believed in an almighty state were not only the totalitarians, like the Nazis and the communists, but also, for instance, US President Franklin Delano Roosevelt, with his New Deal, and the Western democracies that created welfare states and fought unemployment, poverty and hunger after the Second World War. Today, this is no longer possible. If you compare the Great Depression of the 1930s with the financial crisis of 2007/8, the difference is clear. When I was young, we argued over what needed to be done. Today, the main question is who would be able to do it.

Back then, state, capital and labour seem to have formed a sort of stable triangle.

During the period of the mutual dependence of labour and capital, the role of the state was to facilitate the exchange process between the two social partners. The state felt obliged to preserve the labour force as an attractive commodity for potential buyers. That meant subsidizing education, healthcare, housing and so on. This division of responsibility benefitted all three actors, and, if someone had asked them, they probably would have said of this arrangement what Churchill said of democracy: that it was the worst solution, apart from all the others. But the truce between capital and labour, presided over by the state, came to an abrupt end. Many reasons for that collapse have been suggested, but the unilateral cancellation by the bosses of the mutuality of the capital–labour dependency – triggered by globalization but zealously aided and abetted by the state dismantling, one by one, constraints imposed on the capitalists' greed, and the framework and fabric of its victims' defensibility – seems to be the prime contender for utmost pride of place.[19]

What happened to the belief in a strong state?

In the seventies, the state became unpopular because it wasn't able to live up to its promises. The welfare state was in terminal decline. It lacked resources, and people were fed up of the state deciding everything, depriving them of their freedom. The rate of inflation shot up to dizzying heights; unemployment rose. Post-war Europe was built on the fundamental promise of full employment. That was the substance of politics: we must be able to give a job to everyone who needs one. For a while, this went very well. Between 1945 and 1970, social inequality declined, and the low-level unemployment that persisted was considered to be a hangover from earlier years. The post-war period was an exceptional one. When it ended, when unemployment rose and social inequality grew, the state was no longer seen as a saviour. But the situation was still not as dramatic as the one we are in today. The hopes placed in the state were dashed, but there was a replacement, a substitute ideology, and that was the market. Let us unleash the forces of the market, remove obstacles and regulations, move from stability to flexibility, and a miracle will happen – so the idea ran. The market will find what our politicians have been unable to find: the definitive solutions to social problems. Do you remember Margaret Thatcher, Ronald Reagan? Neoliberal opinion-makers, such as the American economist Milton Friedman and the British politician Keith Joseph, were the leading voices, while those sounding early warnings about the dangers and potential conflicts inherent in the new ideology, such as the British sociologist Frank Parkin or the American economist and historian Robert Heilbroner, were not heard. Deregulate, privatize, leave everything to the invisible hand of the market and everything will be fine – that was the thinking.

The recent financial crisis has shaken this trust, too.

Post-war reconstruction, economic growth, near-full employment under the aegis of the state – all this worked very well for thirty years, from the forties to the seventies. And the neoliberal ideology of market domination also worked very well for thirty years. We were all bewitched by it. We gratefully accepted each new credit card offer the postman delivered to us; we were able to spend money that we did not have. They stuffed our mouths with credit cards. That's how well it worked. But, of course, as with any magical solution, it had its limits. And thus, our second great hope was lost too. The collapse of the credit system and the banks in 2007/8 differs from the crises of the thirties and seventies in that we now believe neither in the state nor in the market. That is why I call this period an interregnum, in Antonio Gramsci's – modern – sense of the term. He defined an interregnum as a period in which all the old ways of doing something no longer work, but the new ways have not yet been invented. That is the situation we are in today. All we know is that neither state nor market is capable of repairing the damage that they themselves have caused. Both need to be reined in – that much is clear. But we do not know how they are to be reined in. Uncontrolled markets are dangerous, and the state is impotent. The main question is: who will do what needs to be done? This presents a serious and deepening crisis both for socialist utopians and for advocates of various competing social policy programmes.

But there is also continual rebellion against this stasis.

In his 2008 novel *Diary of a Bad Year*, the South African writer J. M. Coetzee wrote that the traditional choice between 'placid servitude on the one hand and revolt against servitude on the other' has been discarded in favour of an attitude, 'chosen by thousands and millions', that he calls 'quietism' – that is, total passivity, 'willed obscurity' and 'inner emigration'.[20] This tendency, I think, derives from the breakdown of communication between the elite and the rest of the population. The discourses of state politics, on the one hand, and the politics of the common people, on the other, run parallel to each other, and they come into contact only for fleeting moments. At those points, anger and bitterness erupt, and the spark of a usually extinguished political engagement flares up for a moment.

What about the protests of the anti-globalization movement and the Occupy movement, which we often see in the headlines?

People take to the streets and sit in parks or public squares for weeks, and hope that they can occupy Wall Street. Everyone took note of it. The only place that did not take note of it was Wall Street. Wall Street carries on just as before. We have not found anything that works. For that reason, my view is very bleak, but then again, we have never been in this kind of situation before. History has seen many crises, but there was always a conviction that, if we change this or that, everything will be all right again. But I cannot see what this antidote would be. That is what bothers me. We know what we do not want. We are running away from something that does not work. But we do not know where we are heading.

What might be the starting point?

A recently published book by the American sociologist Benjamin Barber, with the provocative title *If Mayors Ruled the World*, is very stimulating. Barber's idea is simple. The necessary changes cannot be made at the level of the state or at the level of 'life politics'. The nation state, which emerged out of the Peace of Westphalia in 1648, was an instrument for gaining independence. Our problem today, however, is that we are all dependent on each other, and the sovereign territorial state is not capable of addressing interdependent problems. The same is true of life politics, which burdens the individual with the responsibility for dealing with social problems. Life politics cannot solve planetary problems because neither you nor I, and not even the mega-rich, have the necessary resources.

So who will save us?

Barber's answer is: the mayors of the big cities. For the first time in history, more than half of the earth's population live in cities; in developing countries, the figure is even as high as 70 per cent. Big cities are situated between state and individual. They have exactly the right dimensions, the population density and ethnic mix, to allow them to mediate between community and society.

'Society' stands for anonymous, bureaucratic relationships, and 'community' for eye-contact and co-operation. The problems faced by cities may be difficult, but they can be tackled empirically. The inhabitants of a city can reach an agreement together. That is Barber's hope. He is not offering a model of the good life, but asking: who might actually be capable of doing something? He suggests creating a world parliament made up of mayors, which would have the aim not of enforcing decisions but of exchanging experiences. This should take priority over all other issues.

In your work, you always come back to the question of responsibility: the responsibility of the individual for her fellow human beings – her 'neighbours', in the Christian sense – as well as responsibility for those who are geographically distant from us but on whose lives we have an immediate influence.

Technology has radically changed our capacity to exert influence, but our moral maturity is still at the level of Adam and Eve's. And that is the problem. We should be aware that we must take on responsibility for something without knowing what it is. We cannot calculate it. That, by the way, is a further development of an idea of Jean-Paul Sartre's. He was the first to say that, in every moment of our lives, we take responsibility without knowing what we are taking responsibility for. We are condemned to have a conscience, which is one of the sources of pain in our lives.

In a globalized world, the scope of our responsibility comes to be as broad as the world itself.

We are already caught in a cosmopolitical situation. We are all connected with each other and dependent on each other. Physical distance does not play as big a role as it used to. Space has come to resemble time. When you think about how far it is from London to Addis Ababa, you do not think in kilometres but in hours. The flight takes seven hours and twenty minutes. When I was offered the sociology chair at the University of Canberra in Australia, I asked one of my colleagues there how far Canberra is from Sydney. His answer was: 10 dollars. That was the price of a plane ticket at the time. I was astounded. He was thinking about it in completely different terms. I wanted him to tell me how many kilometres it is. He didn't even tell me how long it takes. Time wasn't of the essence, but money was. Although we are already in a cosmopolitical situation, we have not yet begun to develop a cosmopolitical mindset. We do not think in cosmopolitical terms but translate things into concepts with which we are familiar. How many dollars, how many hours, does it take?

It is quite an easy thing to say that you are a cosmopolitan, but to be a true citizen of the world is difficult, if not impossible. What would it feel like to be a citizen of humankind, which is, after all, not the same as being a citizen of a polis, a city state in the ancient Greeks' sense?

When you are asked to define yourself, your identity, I do not think that you will say, 'I am a human being, a member of humankind.' We have not begun to grasp the logic of the situation in which we find ourselves. But it is not the first time in humanity's history that a threshold of this kind has been reached. The hunters and gatherers of long ago lived in small tribes. To them, the concept of a 'human being' would have meant a group of around 150 people.[21] The group could not have been larger without ceasing to survive. Without cars or bicycles, or even just horses, the amount of food that the members of a group can gather to keep themselves alive until the next day is limited. There is only a certain amount of fruit, nuts and wild animals to be had. With the invention of agriculture, the groups grew in size and new tribes formed. That was a decisive development that took place before the threshold to modern times was reached. Out of small, face-to-face communities whose members all knew one another developed what the political scientist Benedict Anderson called 'imagined communities'. With this development, an important threshold was crossed, because it involved a transition from a sense of personal identity based in everyday, sensual experience, to one based in abstract concepts. The nations that gradually formed over the course of centuries are such 'imagined communities'. We thus belong to things that exist only in our minds. We never meet in person the vast majority of those who also belong to this community. They are strangers to us, but we identify with their fate, their ideas and the way they view things. That was the decisive step forwards – the transition from *Gemeinschaft* to *Gesellschaft*, in Ferdinand Tönnies's terms.

And you think that today we are facing a similar transition?

We have a no less difficult transition ahead of us: a threshold that we must cross as we have all the thresholds in the past. They were achievements, these passages. But there was something true of all those transitions which is not true of the transition to a cosmopolitical mindset. Each of them created new communities of belonging through opposition to other communities. Germany only came to be formed out of all these principalities because there were both the Germans and the French. 'I am a German' meant, among other things, 'I am not a Frenchman.' In Bavaria, this caused a problem, because the Bavarians were not sure whether they were Germans or Frenchmen. But with the passage ahead of us, there is no outside point of reference, no opposite number. Humankind is humankind; there is no one beyond it.

This is why Planet Earth being attacked by a species of aggressive extraterrestrials is such a popular motif in science fiction: nothing would bind humanity together like a common enemy.

We are in a novel situation because not only is humankind larger than the imagined community of the nation, it is also an inclusive community. A nation state, no matter how large, has its borders. Humankind does not have borders. Everyone who is a member of the species *Homo sapiens* can claim his or her rights as a member of this community. That creates great difficulties. I do not believe that humankind will unite in the near future. The trends point in the opposite direction. People are afraid of the damaging effects of globalization, and rightly so, because these effects are outside their control. Thus, they instinctively withdraw, pull up the drawbridge. However high the price, however much you suffer, however much you are humiliated, at least you, unlike others, are part of the imagined community of this nation state. Hannah Arendt asked what the French Revolution, the Declaration of the Rights of Man and Citizen, really meant. She points out that the declaration did not discuss the rights of every human being, but the rights of every person who was a French citizen. The stateless have no civil rights. Unlike you and me, they can be kept in camps. We have these rights because we are citizens of nations that guarantee them to all their citizens.

And we want to defend these privileges.

That is the problem. I cannot say how this is going to work itself out. I am simply trying to think through the complexity of the task that lies ahead of us. Yes, on the one hand, humanity has taken great steps forwards several times in its history. But, on the other hand, we have reached the end of the road. What is being asked of us is completely novel: to say 'I am a citizen of the world', while at the same time to resist the thought that my fellow citizens seem alien to me. I can no longer choose them. Everyone is entitled to be a member of this comprehensive community of all human beings. That has never been the case before.

*We are all in the same boat – or, rather, we should say,
'spaceship'. Spaceship Earth, alone in the universe.*

We understand this in theory, but we are very far from
behaving accordingly – from acting as if we really were
sitting in a spaceship together.

*The intellectual's task is to insist on the need to move in
that direction. The French philosophers, the intellectuals
of the Enlightenment, once were the dominant voices in
Europe, as you explain in your* Legislators and Interpreters
of 1987. *But today – we touched upon this before – there
are hardly any politicians, entrepreneurs or other power
brokers listening to intellectuals.*

This is an enormously important problem. When, in a
short while, I shall die – because I am a very old man – I
shall die unfulfilled and unhappy, because I wrestled with
a question in order to find a convincing answer, and I did
not succeed. I know that I shall not find the answer now
– I have no time left. It is a simple question: how do you
make the world new? That question comes from scripture,
the New Testament: 'Behold, I make all things new', Jesus
is quoted as saying in the Book of Revelation.[22] I have
studied all that has been written on this theme, on the
question of how one turns words into deeds. All philosophers talk about it, but I have not found a single answer
that has satisfied me. Throughout the course of my life,
this question has become more and more important to me.
I think it is now more urgent than ever before. Today, at
the end of my life, that is my greatest worry.

What do you see as sociology's task today?

Under these conditions, sociology acquires a new,
enormously important public sphere, and that is the
community of individuals – individuals who find themselves
confronted with very obscure, nebulous, extraterritorial

worlds. I try to explain the mechanism behind this, to understand what is taking place. That is the precondition for an individual to attempt to take control of his or her life. I do not say that you will be successful in this; I do not give advice. But one should at least become more knowledgeable, should know what takes place behind the phenomena. Sociology, to me, means making the familiar unfamiliar and the unfamiliar familiar. That is sociology's task. I do not think that sociology is in crisis. I think sociologists are needed more than ever – a new generation of sociologists for the present generation.

The concept of a 'generation', articulated by the Spanish philosopher José Ortega y Gasset, is barely a century old. What does it mean today?

Its emergence goes back to the devastating experience of the Great War, which split the generations apart from one another. The rupture in European identity caused by this war made the concept of a 'generation' one of the most important tools for investigating social and political divides. 'Generation' is an objective scientific category that rests on differences between subjective life experiences. Today, for various reasons, the experiences which define a generation do not play a role – or play only a minor role – among the generation that comes after them.

Didn't the ancient Greeks already complain about 'today's youth'? Socrates said they have 'bad manners' and 'disrespect for their elders' and that they 'love chatter in place of exercise'.[23] Maybe different generations resemble one another more than we usually think.

The earliest traces of generational conflict can be found in antiquity, but it only fully breaks out in modernity. This is because modernity brings with it the belief that the world can be changed, and changed through human intervention, and because the world begins to be transformed at such a pace that a single lifetime is long enough for someone to be able to say 'things used to be different'; and, moreover, because there is a distinction made between 'is' and 'ought', and between the 'good old days' and a 'better future'.

What does this mean for community?

The idea of a community has been replaced with the idea of a network. A community is difficult to join. Not everyone can become Swiss. It involves long, drawn-out procedures. Leaving a community is also difficult. If you want to break off human ties, you need considerable ingenuity. You have to come up with reasons; you have to negotiate. And even if you are successful, you never know whether there may be drawbacks, and if so when these might make themselves felt. In the case of social networks, on Facebook, that is different. It is easy to join and participate, and just as easy to leave. 'Network' is a trendy way of describing a totality that differs from a community of the past, which a person was born into, had a place in, and was condemned to remain in for the rest of his or her life. In a network, the opposite is the case. If I don't like it, I can reshape it. If I don't like someone, I can ignore them, by not answering or blocking their messages. The only person who will notice is them, because the network does not control how I behave. The network might not even be aware of my presence. Where the community eyed you with suspicion, noting every misdeed, and had at its disposal a long list of means for sanctioning and punishing deviant behaviour, a network lacks these options. It is as malleable as plasticine.

How does this influence 'real' communities, such as associations or interest groups?

They are being reshaped by this development, just as relationships are being reshaped by online dating. Hardly any community today makes a demand on the whole human being; every human being has several affiliations. Thus, it is also no longer seen as a betrayal of the community to serve up one's loyalty *à la carte*, so to speak. Integrative communities are today almost exclusively to be found among those at the bottom end of the sociocultural ladder. There, human ties are still something meant for life, as was generally the case in previous times.

Religion and Fundamentalism

The end of the world: why it is important to believe in (a non-existent) God

In your book Liquid Surveillance, *you say our age is defined by fear. In seeking to protect us against it, society produces more of it. Weren't the fears of previous times even worse – the fear of God, the Devil, hell, ghosts, nature?*

I do not believe that people's fears are greater today than they were in earlier times. But they are different: more arbitrary, diffuse, nebulous. You work for a company for thirty years. You are held in high esteem. Suddenly a corporation comes along, swallows up your company and starts asset-stripping it. You are fired. If you are 50 years old, your chances of finding a new job are slim. Many people today live in fear of this sort of thing. It comes out of nowhere, and it is impossible to take precautions against it.

And in the past, this was different?

You were afraid of something concrete. The crops were failing. You looked up at the sky: would it rain, or would it remain dry, leaving everything to wilt and rot? The children had to walk to school, but along the way was a small forest inhabited by a wolf, so they had to be accompanied. Even when we feared nuclear war, people believed that they could protect themselves by building a bunker. Of course, that was silly, but the thought was that you were still able to do something. You did not despair. You told yourself: 'I am a good person. I will build an air-raid shelter for my family.'

But we in the wealthy countries of the world live longer, more secure lives today than anyone has lived before. After all, the risks we face have diminished significantly.

We have to distinguish the concept of risk from the concept of danger in order to illustrate the difference I have in mind. A danger is something specific: you know what it is you are afraid of, and you can take precautions. This is not the case with risk. Many thinkers have noted the paradox that today we are far more secure than ever before, yet at the same time haunted by feelings of insecurity.

Feelings that drive an entire industry.

The security industry is the growth industry par excellence, the only sector that is completely immune to the effects of economic crisis. That success has nothing to do with statistics or facts about actual threats. International terrorism is a very good pretext for deploying security measures, developing security technology and toughening up the security apparatus. The number of victims of international terrorism is ridiculously small compared to the number of road deaths. So many people die on the roads, and the media don't even talk about it.

Every car should have a sticker on it like the warnings on cigarette packs: 'Driving a car harms your health and the health of those around you.'

Yes, exactly! On the other hand, the standard of living has risen. In our part of the world we no longer need to worry about our daily bread. Still, since the financial crisis, people are increasingly fearful of falling into poverty. The whole middle class is now subject to the vicissitudes of the market and fears that its standard of living will drop for good. And that's not to mention the workers who have lost their jobs. For sure, the standard of living is far higher than it was in the nineteenth century, but somehow it no longer makes us happy. Even after gratifying, pleasurable days, many people go to bed and have nightmares. The devils they repress during their busy working day come out in the stillness of the night, when all their fears bubble up to the surface.

You have said that depression is the characteristic psychological affliction of consumer society.

In the past, we were weighed down by an overabundance of prohibitions. Our neuroses were caused by the terror of guilt, the fear of being accused of breaking the rules. Today, we suffer from an excess of possibility. We are terrified of being inadequate. That is the fear that underlies depression.

And even when it does not lead to depression, it leads to an obsession with security.

Fear is the most insidious of all the demons of our open society. We may be spoiled. We may seem to be well. But we feel threatened, insecure, anxious, prone to panic. That is why we are obsessed with security to a much greater extent than most societies before us. Uncertainty, about both the present and the future, gives rise to fears that simply overwhelm us. You write that we need scapegoats in order to give a form to these fears, or words to that effect. Today's fears differ from those of earlier epochs in that there is now no longer any connection between the causes of the fears and the actions that are taken to protect ourselves against them. We find substitute objects to discharge our unmanageable excess existential fear. We flee from second-hand smoke, fatty foods, too much exposure to sunlight, unprotected sex. [*Bauman reaches for his pipe.*] Do you mind if I smoke?

No, not at all.

You are not afraid of passive smoking?

No.

It bothers my wife, Aleksandra. Janina smoked all her life – there was no problem there. But Aleksandra minds because she was never a smoker.

Do you smoke cigarettes too?

I have to, because smoking pipes is a full-time job. Smoking cigarettes is much easier. I sit in front of my computer, compose something and – you probably know the feeling – suddenly, in the middle of a sentence, I no longer know how to go on, how to conclude the sentence.

So you reach for a cigarette.

Cigarettes are no good because they are finished after a few puffs. Smoking pipes is a serious business: you have to clean the pipe, fill it with tobacco, light it, and then relight it again and again when it goes out. And while I do all this, the end of the sentence comes to me – just like that.

What was the turning point? When did the old-style fears give way to the new fears, like the fear of second-hand smoke?

Those specifically modern fears appeared when deregu-lation and individualization ripped apart – or at least considerably weakened – the traditional bonds of community, those bonds between relatives and neighbours which had existed since time immemorial and seemed as though they would last forever. With the disintegration of communities, fears were also individualized. The pervasive sense of insecurity today leaves everyone alone with their fears.

When discussing ethical questions, you often refer to religion. You touch on themes that others usually leave to the theologians: evil, moral responsibility, the value of long-term relationships, self-sacrifice, brotherly love, death. Sometimes, it almost seems as if you are a secret theologian.

I must confess that I am not a religious man myself. But, in the course of my life, I have gradually come to see the importance of religion, the significance of faith and transcendence. Without religion, I think, humaneness is inconceivable. We cannot all be saints, but if there were no holy people among us, we would not even be human. They show us the way. They demonstrate to us that the way is a possibility for us. And they prick our conscience when we refuse to acknowledge that and refuse to take that way. We, too, look to something larger than ourselves. If it is not God, then it is something else – the pursuit of profit, the cult of money or the technology we fetishize so much these days.

Apart from the fundamentalist movements in Islam and Christianity, has there been a broader religious revival?

In the Western world, what we are seeing is a revival not of religion but of spirituality. People are not flocking back to the churches, but they are turning inwards, to something beyond ordinary life and everyday concerns. Did you read my two little books that were recently published, the conversations with Stanisław Obirek?

I have On the World and Ourselves *lying on my bedside table.*

The other is called *Of God and Man.* Stanisław Obirek is a brilliant man, very erudite. He was a Jesuit and a practising priest. He is no longer either, but he is still a sincere Catholic. He left the institution, but not the idea. That is something we share. I was never a Jesuit, but I was a communist. I left the party just as he left the Church. I remained faithful to my moral principles and to the socialist ideal.

In On the World and Ourselves, *you talk about these transitions, these rites of passage. Stanisław Obirek criticized the Roman Catholic Church in Poland and was forced by the provincial superior to keep silent for a year as punishment. He then left the order. Unlike him, you are not religious, but you do consider religion to be indispensable. How does that fit together?*

All of my thoughts on religion rest on the conviction that God will perish together with humankind. To put it differently, I believe that humankind is inconceivable without the idea of God. With this claim, I pick up a thought from my late friend Leszek Kołakowski, who said that God stands for the inadequacy of human beings. Our capacities are not adequate to the challenges confronting us, and inevitably we recognize this. It is obvious. But modernity questions this human inadequacy. It declares that science and technology will allow us to overcome our weaknesses. They are only temporary, it is claimed, and not a fundamental characteristic of human nature: we have not yet arrived at 'Salomon's House'. If we try hard enough, spend enough on research, we will get there, and we will thus have transcended the humiliating feeling that the human species is inadequate.

Kołakowski wrote that the 'self-deification of mankind, to which Marxism gave philosophical expression ... has

revealed itself as the farcical aspect of human bondage'.[24]
Today, it is probably only among the Silicon Valley vision-
aries, and among others who think 'faith in science' is
a good thing, that one finds a belief that humanity can
surpass itself and create a paradise on earth.

We no longer believe that things will turn towards the
good. We have transitioned to a new kind of inadequacy:
the inadequacy of the individual who is expected to solve
the problems that were hitherto matters for government,
state and community – in other words, expected to find a
bearable place in a world that cannot be improved. The
world is doomed, but each individual must find her own
solutions amid this social decline.

You mentioned 'Salomon's House', Francis Bacon's name
for the research institute in his New Atlantis *of 1627,*
which encapsulates his vision of future discovery and
knowledge. What shattered the belief in the possibility of
creating an ideal society and controlling nature?

I think it began in 1755, with the catastrophe of Lisbon:
an earthquake, a major fire, a tsunami – three catastrophes
in one. It was one of the most devastating natural disasters
in European history. It made an enormous impression
on Europe's intelligentsia, because Lisbon was one of the
centres of civilization and the Enlightenment. What it made
clear was that nature did not obey our moral principles.
Misfortune befell the virtuous and the vicious alike. It could
not have been a divine response to sin, because sinners and
the innocent alike were killed, accidentally and at random.
Still, we affirmed our decision to place the world under
human management. We cannot expect God to manage it,
because his creation, nature, is altogether blind. We can't
trust it. We must take things into our own hands, and with
the help of science and technology we shall bring everything
under control. Humanity is still inadequate, but it is only
a matter of time until that will change. That was the idea.

The destructive power and bountiful potential of nature led so-called primitive cultures to ask the gods for protection and help. Rain dances, for instance – ceremonies intended to bring on rain and so protect the harvest – were widespread in ancient Egypt, among Native Americans, and in the Balkans as late as the twentieth century.

People were aware that they had no control over nature. They believed in a higher power, and they prayed and offered sacrifices in the hope that this higher power would pardon and protect them. They sensed their inadequacy, and they knew that, as humans, it was not within their power to prevent catastrophe and to ensure a prosperous life just by their own efforts. But our sense of individual inadequacy today, in the twenty-first century, is of a different sort. It does not necessarily give rise to religion.

But many people, especially in modern societies, believe in the supernatural. People believe in all sorts of hocus-pocus.

Stanisław Obirek wrote a wonderful book, *God of My Own*, in which he discusses this revival of non-institution-alized religion. This is not a church-based religion with a single God, in which all members of the congregation believe. People are looking for an individual God – that is, a God of their own. They construct this god out of various elements: this from the Jewish Cabbala, that from Buddhism, yet another thing from Christianity – wherever they can find a comforting, even if illusory, sense of a haven from the storm. Both the traditional, church-based religions and this 'God of my own' involve a God. That is the common denominator. But in terms of social practice, they are very different phenomena.

Traditional religion involves community; the modern is egocentric.

More and more people are desperately trying to find

something that is greater than themselves, but it is also meant to be user-friendly. Because they are responsible for finding individual solutions to social problems, they also feel responsible for creating their own God. They do not expect that God to be offered to them on a silver platter. It is no longer a matter of going to church once a week. It is a different ball game, as the Americans would put it: an altogether different matter. There does not necessarily have to be religion, but if there is to be a religion, then it must be a religion with an individual God.

What is the significance of the rise of fundamentalism? What is the connection between a form of fundamentalism and the particular religion it claims to represent in its pure form?

Fundamentalism can be expressed in religious terms, not only in the case of conflicts between different religions, such as Islam and Christianity, but also in the case of conflicts within a single religion, as in the case of Shi'ites and Sunnis in Islam. The apparent revival of religion is not a revival of the major faiths themselves, but of sectarianism. What is taking place in the Middle East is a battle within Islam. But I would not hold religion responsible for the increasing levels of aggression, break-downs in communication, hopelessness, division, erection of borders and violence we are seeing. Religion, which is based on humankind's inadequacy as such, is used as an argument by individuals and networks who want to overcome their own concrete inadequacies. That is the core of fundamentalism.

Your engagement with religious questions suggests to me that you are not yourself an atheist, but neither do you seem to be a believer. Are you an agnostic?

I think I am an atheist: I do not believe that there is such a thing as a personal God. But I do believe that God is indispensable to our survival. I can't imagine humanity living without God. The human being is an intelligent animal. Unlike animals, humans realize that they are inadequate – that they lack something. However bold we might be, we also come up against limits and question what lies behind them.

But this experience does not necessarily lead to faith. In your case, at least, it clearly has not.

There are two ideas that are objectively impossible to grasp: infinity and nothingness. You cannot imagine nothingness, because if you imagine nothing you are present in the act of imagining. It is impossible to imagine nothingness without including oneself in it, so it is not nothingness. Imagining it is beyond our conceptual faculties. The same is true of infinity. All our experiences are bound up with time. Infinity is not just something that lasts an extraordinarily long time; it is something without beginning and without end. The idea of the Big Bang, the beginning of infinity, leads to the question of what was there before. The greatest cosmologists can tell you every detail of exactly what happened in the seconds after the Big Bang ...

... Steven Weinberg, the Nobel laureate, wrote a nice book about it, The First Three Minutes ...

... but when you ask them what came before, they fall silent. It is rare for someone to discover God because of this problem, because questions about infinity and nothingness are, in principle, philosophical questions. I can well understand a philosopher having sleepless nights over them, but I do not believe that anyone else, any non-philosophers, will get a headache from them. All I want to say is that there is good reason for this feeling that there is a force, a higher being, a God. There are limits to our understanding. These limits may be drawn in different ways for different people, but they are always there. To reiterate: God will die, but humanity will die along with Him.

What you say is paradoxical: you are an atheist, but you are also convinced that humanity will die along with God.

I don't think that it is a paradox. It is part of being human. We have all sorts of important traits, among them the fact that our thinking and acting inevitably forces us to confront our inadequacies, which, in turn, leads us to believe that there must be something else, something above us, a force that holds everything together. I am a human being, and, because I am a human being, my faculty of understanding is limited. The limitation indicates the existence of something beyond this limitation. The demand for religion is thus being produced all of the time, by all of us. We do not need priests to do it for us. It is spontaneous. I do not see this as a paradox.

How can you consider faith essential and yet not believe yourself?

Let me illustrate this with a comparison. At the beginning of our conversation, I said that in the story of my life I am not an ornithologist; I am a bird. But in the story of my life as a scientist, as a sociologist, it is the other way around: here, I am not a bird, but an ornithologist. Ornithologists study birds, but I have never heard of a bird that has become an ornithologist. I study religion, try to understand why it has never, throughout the whole of human history, disappeared. Even among the first primitive tribes, some form of religion was present, and anthropologists who have travelled the world over have not found a single human group lacking an idea of the supernatural. The belief is always there, in every period, even if in different forms and even if not held by every individual.

That humanity will go the way of the dinosaurs is a

dystopian prospect. For most people, the idea is associated not with God but with the worry that we ourselves will destroy the planet.

The astronomers still give us 5 billion years. Then the sun will explode, turn into a red giant and finally collapse into a white dwarf. But the end of the world as we know it may come much earlier. The news about the consequences of global warming is becoming ever more horrifying. A rise in global temperatures of half a per cent, I read somewhere, would be enough to leave us without food. The German sociologist and social psychologist Harald Welzer has an interesting book called *Climate Wars*.[25] He predicts that in the twenty-first century, our century, people will not die because of ideological conflict but because of food scarcity and poor living conditions. Suddenly, the most densely populated areas of the earth will become the places people are least able to feed themselves. In large parts of the world, he says, climate change will lead to a collapse of the social and political order and 'never-ending war'.

Utopia and History

Time travel: where is 'the beyond' today?

There are countless dystopias today, but few utopias.
While the former paint pictures of hell, the latter seek
heaven on earth. Most utopian plans remained words on
paper, but communism, which you yourself believed in,
has influenced the world to an unparalleled extent. Are
alternative, utopian concepts of society now obsolete?

One of my first publications of the British part of my
academic life carried the title *Socialism: The Active Utopia*,
which signalled its main message: the great historical
accomplishment of the socialist idea was its acting as a
utopia laying bare the social ills endemic in the status quo
and spurring remedial action. Without the presence of such
a utopia, those ills would grow and proliferate uncontrol-
lably, with the moral standards of society, together with
quality of life, bound to become the first, and perhaps
the most regrettable, collateral victim of that growth.
(Inadvertently, that old belief was to be retrospectively
confirmed by the story of the Western societies after the
fall of the Berlin Wall.) What derived from that message
was another belief: that declaring any kind of status quo
as the 'socialist idea fulfilled' cannot but be a death knell
to what was its major, indeed paramount, role to be played

in history. In the longer run, such a declaration would have inevitably stripped the socialist utopia of that role. The same applies to current thinking about democracy, because democracy is also a utopia, an ideal condition that has not yet been established.

After the historical political turn of 1989, the collapse of the Soviet empire, people frequently spoke of the 'end of ideologies'. If we leave aside neoliberalism and neoconservatism, that is, in a certain sense, correct: ideologies of social reform have also become obsolete.

That's true, but the end of ideology is still further away than ever. Modernity was based on the conviction that everything can be perfected through the exercise of human capacities. But the maxim of today's politics is: there is no alternative. That is what the higher powers tell the people: any rational reflection on the social order is a waste of time. According to the new ideology of privatization, such reflection contributes nothing to the good life. Work more and earn more money, but do not think about society or do anything for the community – that is what people are told. Margaret Thatcher, the Iron Lady, declared that there is no such thing as society, only individual men, women and families.

To the younger generations, the idea that there is no alternative seems natural.

Many of them have lost the ability to think about the good society. They prefer to think about how to find a comfortable niche – for themselves, their families, their relatives – in this disorderly, unpredictable and uncomfortable world. That's no great surprise: we live in a multicultural, multi-centred world, a world of uncertainty. Long-term planning is no use because everything is changing so quickly. We have no lodestar. The idea of the good society no longer figures in public debate. At best, we have the idea of a society that is a little less bad than the present one. Politicians who present themselves as 'strong leaders', like Donald Trump, Viktor Orbán or Marine Le Pen, do not offer people an alternative society. They claim to be the alternative personified.

You describe the historical development of utopian thinking using the metaphors of the gamekeeper, the gardener and the hunter. The premodern attitude towards the world was that of a gamekeeper, while the modern attitude was that of a gardener. Now, in the postmodern era, the attitude of the hunter has come to dominate. How does this sort of utopian thinking differ from earlier modern attitudes?

It's no longer about conservation and maintenance. It is not about the creation of beautiful gardens, as it used to be. Today, all people care about is filling up their own hunting bag, with no concern for the remaining supply of game. Social historians discuss this transformation under the heading of 'individualization', while politicians promote it as 'deregulation'. Unlike earlier utopias, the utopia of the hunter doesn't imbue life with any meaning, either real or spurious. It merely serves to banish questions about the meaning of life from people's minds.

What are the foundations of this utopia? It is, after all, supposed to provide us with hope.

We're dealing with two mutually complementary utopias here: the one of the free market's wondrous healing power, and the other of the infinite capacity of the technological fix. Both are anarchic. They envisage a world with rights, but also without duties and, above all, without rulers. They militate against any plan, against the delay of gratification, against sacrifices on behalf of future benefits. The spontaneity of the world conjured up here makes a nonsense of all concerns about the future – except the concern about being free from all concerns about the future and so being allowed to act without having to care about anything.

Even if we no longer have any positive ideas about how the future might be, can we not at least learn from history? As Cicero said, history is 'life's teacher'.

The idea that 'Historia magistra vitae est' – history is life's teacher – has fallen victim to our increasing gloominess about the future in general, and progress in particular. Most people have found their hopes frustrated. The pace of change has accelerated, and even people who are much younger than I am have experienced a whole variety of unfulfilled promises, abandoned plans and disappointed hopes. When I was young, a child, a teenager, people believed that the future would be one of continual improvement. Every year would be better than the year before, and we would learn from history not to repeat the mistakes of the past. We would develop better technologies, better ways and means of doing the right thing. The future, we believed, was a path that was leading up, not down.

In ancient Greek and Roman mythology, it was precisely the other way around: history began with the golden age, and it was all downhill from there – to the silver and bronze ages, and so on, right up to the disaster of their present, the iron age, which was a condition of decline and decay.

With the onset of modernity, people began to believe that things would improve and develop into a new golden age. They dreamt of a perfect society. Leon Battista Alberti, the 'uomo universale' of the Renaissance, said that a perfect society would be a condition in which any further change could only be a deterioration. People thought that, having learned so much from our mistakes, having become so wise and having developed such fine technology, we would ultimately create such an ideal condition. Perfection means the impossibility of further improvement, the end of history. The belief was that, with the creation of this perfect society, people would finally be able to relax and to reap the rewards of the efforts of the preceding generations. No one in their right mind expects this today. But maybe we should concern ourselves less with our past mistakes and more with old ideas that were ignored, discarded or simply forgotten in the past. It is possible that such ideas might contain the seed of something better than what we have today.

Have we at least come to an understanding of our present predicament?

I do not believe anyone has a consistent theory of what is going on right now. We are groping around in the dark. My new book is not a precise description of the present either; it is not an attempt to capture current trends or to suggest what might be coming. As I already mentioned, its title is *Retrotopia* – a portmanteau of the fashionable word 'retro' and the word 'utopia'. Utopias have always been situated in the future, but the future is no longer attractive. It is full of risks, dangers and challenges. It is unpredictable and uncontrollable, an era of the uncertain. We do not know which direction things will go in, so we do not know which preventive measures should be taken or what we should do in the present moment. We have lost trust in the idea of progress; it is no longer a cheering thought, but an anxiety-inducing one. It makes me anxious, too. I will not be able to keep abreast of the changes. I may well become superfluous, my profession redundant. So many trades and professions have already become automated. Car factories now contain hardly any workers. Have you heard the joke about the factory of the future?

No.

In the factory of the future, there will be only two living creatures left: a man and a dog. The man's job will be to feed the dog, and the dog's job will be to make sure that the man does not touch anything. The joke captures a widespread feeling. Jobs are disappearing all the time, replaced not by human competitors but by computers and robots. There are also worrying signs that intellectual labour will become automated.

You said utopias are located in the future. To what, then, does the 'retro' in the title of your book refer?

Today, many people think that the paradise of stability and security lies in the past. That is the home they long for. People are now writing utopias of the past. But there is no public awareness of the fact that the dividing line between past and future has been erased. There is practically no difference, no existential or ontological difference, between future and past. When I was young, a long time ago, everyone said the future was the realm of the unknown and of freedom, and the past was the realm of stability and unfreedom.

Although we know a great deal about what happened in the past, there always remains plenty of room for speculation. Like the ideas of the future, those of the past are also, more or less, fictions.

In his *1984*, George Orwell predicted how this fact could be put to use politically. In the totalitarian state he describes, the 'Ministry of Truth' controls the past in order to control the thoughts of its subjects. Today, this is called the 'politics of history' or the 'politics of memory', a phenomenon that has become widespread in many European countries. My suspicion is that what underlies this trend among politicians, this 'politics of history', is the insecurity of the present and the uncertainty of the future. The past is a vast container that holds all sorts of things.

You can pick up whatever happens to suit your purposes and leave the rest. As a result, there are several dozen versions of one and the same history. Historical memory is used selectively to advance particular partisan interests. This is what we are seeing today. It is the opposite of what Leopold von Ranke said historians should do – namely, write down everything 'as it actually happened'.

An impossible thing to do.

Clearly, writing history the way it actually happened is impossible. Every historical narrative is selective; it could not be otherwise. Do you remember Jorge Louis Borges's short story *Funes the Memorious*? As a result of a horse-riding accident, Funes acquires a very strange affliction. He is incapable of generalizing, of making general statements.

But he remembers every single detail of his life.

He cannot understand why a dog that is running falls under the same concept as a dog that is sitting. As a result, he is unable to tell a story, because to tell the story would take exactly as long as the events themselves had taken. That is what is actually happening today. When we think about the future, we can imagine only chaos, because the future contains too many frightening possibilities for us to enumerate them all. And when we look back – hence my 'retro' – it is the same. There is a whole range of things to which we may help ourselves, and whoever, and with whatever intentions, immerses herself in the past will return with a different yield. In *Retrotopia*, I try to bring these ideas into a kind of order. But that is far from easy. José Saramago has written very beautifully about just this. He is one of the novelists I most admire, and he is also, I think, an important philosopher: his novels can be read as philosophical statements. In one of his diary entries, he described a feeling I share. He wrote that, looking back – he was 86 years old at the time – he was sad because he had not been able to share with others the few wise ideas he had had. He had put them forward, but no one had taken them up. They had not exerted any influence. So he asks himself a radical question: why do we think? His answer is that we think just as we sweat. We cannot do anything about it; we can't help it. Well, that is the reason why I think. I can't help it. It is a long – a life-long – training: a drill, really.

What idea are you most preoccupied with?

How words become deeds – that is the problem I can't let go of. How we might confront growing inequality – that is the question closest to my heart. It is a very interesting phenomenon.

Present and Future

Human waste: who are the witches of modern society?

For you, fashion is an example of what consumer society has made of us. Nothing good, right?

Fashion revolves around the idea that everything we buy must soon be discarded. There are good clothes that could still be worn, but, since they are out of fashion, we are ashamed to be seen in them. At the office, the boss looks us over and exclaims, 'How dare you show up dressed liked this?' When children go to school with last year's sneakers, they're subject to ridicule. There's pressure to conform. Paradoxically, those who follow fashion believe that they stand out from the crowd.

Fashion is a relatively harmless example of how consumer society specializes in the production of trash. A more serious matter is what you call the 'production of "human waste"'.[26] Why do you classify the unemployed as rubbish?

Because society no longer has any use for them, and their lives are seen as worthless, just like the lives of refugees. That's the result of globalization, of economic progress.

The number of people who have lost their jobs in the wake of capitalism's triumphant march across the globe continues to rise unabated, and will soon reach the limits of what the earth can handle. With each outpost that the capital markets conquer, the sea of men and women who have been stripped of their land, their property, their jobs and their social safety nets grows by the thousands, or even millions. This creates a new type of underclass, a class of failed consumers. They no longer have a place in society. We no longer know where to put them now that disposal sites are in short supply and the areas to which we used to export surplus workers are no longer available. The success of our welfare-state democracies was for a long time based on this possibility. Today, every last corner of our planet is occupied. That is what's new about the current crisis.

What about the refugees who come to us seeking shelter?

Back in 1950, the official statistics already counted 1 million refugees, most of them so-called 'displaced persons' from the Second World War. Today, according to UN figures, that number has risen to 65 million. By 2050, there will be an estimated 1 billion exiled refugees, shunted into the no man's land of transit camps. Refugees, migrants, the marginalized – there are always more of them.

How do we know this isn't just a temporary phenomenon?

Becoming an inmate of a refugee camp means eviction from the world and from humanity. Refugees are not only surplus, but also superfluous. The path back to their lost homeland is forever barred. The occupants of the camps are robbed of all features of their identity, with one exception: the fact that they are refugees. Without a state, without a home, without a function, without papers. Permanently marginalized, they also stand outside the law. As the French anthropologist Michel Agier notes in his study on refugees in the era of globalization, they are not outside this or that law in this country or another, but outside the law altogether.

Refugee camps, you say, are akin to laboratories in which the new, permanently temporary mode of living of liquid modernity is tested.

In the globalized world, asylum-seekers and so-called economic refugees collectively resemble the new power elite, the finance industry and the large corporations, who are actually the true villains in this drama. Just like this elite, they are not tied to a fixed location. They are erratic and unpredictable.

Today, most warfare, including the most cruel and bloody conflicts, is waged by non-state actors. This deregulation of war, you say, is another sinister consequence of globalization. Who are these actors?

They are the latecomers to modernity. They feel forced to act on their own initiative to find local solutions for global problems. The results are tribal wars, massacres, marauding guerrilla armies and criminal gangs parading as freedom fighters. They slaughter each other, soaking up and simultaneously eliminating the excess population – mostly young people who have no chance of finding work and a future life worth living. That is one of the perverse local solutions for a global problem. In short, this is the poor man's imperialism. Hundreds of thousands of people are chased out of their houses, murdered or expelled from their countries. Perhaps the only flourishing industry in the so-called developing countries, the countries of these latecomers to modernity, is the mass production of refugees.

What could or should governments do about these 'waste products of modernity'?

Governments cannot do anything against the global power elites, and that is why they dedicate themselves to other high-profile issues that allow them to appear efficacious. The essential point is that whatever they do must be within their capabilities. Governments aid and abet popular prejudices because they don't want to confront the genuine sources of existential uncertainty troubling their electors. Asylum-seekers take on the role that was previously reserved for the witches, goblins and ghosts of folklore and legend.

In the course of this development, you say, the welfare-state democracies have become security states. What distinguishes the two?

The welfare state takes a society based on inclusion as its model. The security state does just the opposite. It's about exclusion from society by means of punishment and incarceration. The security industry then becomes responsible for the disposal of human waste. One element of the security state is the for-profit prison sector – for instance, in the USA, the UK, Canada, Australia, Chile and South Africa.

The right-wing parties that are now setting the agenda all across Europe have accelerated this development towards the security state. They're supported by a media that give a platform to people scaremongering about 'overpopulation' and seeking to link the issue of 'asylum' with 'terror'.

The success of radical right-wing parties is based on a visible fact: immigration. And everything gets traced back to it. Why is there unemployment? Because of the immigrants. Why is the education in our schools so bad? Because of immigrants. Why is crime on the rise? Because of immigrants. If only we could send them back where they came from, all our problems would be gone. That's an illusion. There are more important reasons to be afraid than a few thousand – or a few hundred thousand – immigrants. But it works. It's a psychological consolation: 'I know what is bothering me. I have something that I can attach my fears to.'

The immigrant is the lightning conductor for the insecurity caused by the economy.

Not only for that but also for other fears. The illegal immigrant comes to personify all sorts of threats, threats against which the modern state has promised to protect its subjects: serial killers, muggers, stalkers, beggars, paedophiles – whatever. And, of course, terrorists. This underclass is enormously useful to a society in which no profession and no trade is certain of its long-term utility, and thus its long-term market value. Everything can be offloaded onto this underclass. It serves as a safety valve for the built-up anger about the conditions of a society one is unable to change. What are feared most today are human malice and human evildoers.

You paint a gloomy picture of the future. You also find little to like about modern technology – for instance, the internet. But doesn't it have many upsides? Social networks were successfully used by democratic movements such as the Arab Spring. What's the downside?

When it comes to destroying something – toppling a government – it can be useful. The weakness of such movements is that they only have vague plans for the day after. Outraged people are virtually all-powerful as a demolition force. They have yet to show that they are equally capable of building up something new.

The internet has not only enabled global communication – it is also changing the way we communicate.

Today, there is someone somewhere we can get in touch

with twenty-four hours a day, seven days a week. You can always find someone who is sitting in front of a computer. You are never alone. But if you are offline, you have experiences that you cannot have in front of a computer. Walking home from work, you cannot avoid meeting all sorts of people, strangers who look different, behave differently and speak different languages. You become aware that you are surrounded by people who are not like yourself. They do not have the same view of the world or the same ideas as you. Engaging with them requires dialogue. You realize that negotiation is an important task that you somehow must carry out. On the internet, this is not the case. All the research shows that people who communicate via the internet gravitate towards like-minded people. Negotiation is unnecessary because they already more or less agree. They create something that is impossible to create in real life: an echo chamber. All you hear is your own voice echoed back at you. But talking to people who say the same things as you is not dialogue. We can also think of it as a hall of mirrors: wherever you look, you see your own likeness. Those who spend a lot of time on the internet start to ignore the reality that exists beyond their circles of friends. I can appreciate that this is very comforting and soothing. You feel secure. You live under the illusion that you are right and that everyone else is wrong. Those others do exist, but they are not important. And even if you do end up arguing with someone on the internet, you can simply exit. You do not need to negotiate. In real life, it is not so easy. The internet is a tool that brings people together from all over the world, but it also divides people. The partisan trenches it creates are deeper and more difficult to bridge than those in real life, where we can find common ground through compromise and personal engagement.

Technical progress has always led to change in society. Today, however, you say it involves more than that. Why?

Because we are no longer developing technologies simply to find the most appropriate means for our ends. We are instead allowing our goals to be determined by the available means of technology. We don't develop means to do what we want to be done. We do what is made possible by the means. The things that should serve us take us into their service. We are their slaves.

But hasn't that always been the case? From the invention of the wheel to the fission of the atom, technological advances have been used for all sorts of purposes, good and bad.

It's a question of dimension. Of course, technology has always influenced the way we live, and changes have often been met with criticism. This was the case when Gutenberg invented the printing press. Among the educated classes, there was a widely held view that it would lead to moral decay. 'Everyone will learn to read', they complained. They were of the opinion that the lower classes should not be educated, because it would weaken their willingness to work.

But that's also the case with the internet. It's given countless millions of people from poor areas of the world access to education that was previously unavailable to them. So why do you complain?

Historically, the development of technology has tended to occur in small steps. There were innovations here and there, but not on a global scale, not with revolutionary impact, and not in a way that changed all of society and its way of life. Innovations were absorbed and adapted and became part of daily life. Today, it's different. The changes brought about by technology are massive, and they exhibit certain totalitarian tendencies. One of Russia's oligarchs, Dmitry Itskov, launched his '2045 Initiative', a research project that aims to make the human brain superfluous.

He's financing the development of an electronic machine that is intended to think like a human being. Whether it's actually realistic, I can't say. But the fact that someone would have an idea like that is a novelty. For the first time, our thinking is threatened by machines.

You insist that the future can't be predicted. But aren't prognoses important if we are to make the right decisions about what to do here and now?

But predictions are impossible. My favourite example is the story of a now thankfully defunct academic discipline called Sovietology. Sovietology was a unique discipline in the history of academia: the only one never to experience budget cuts. No matter how many chairs Sovietologists wanted to create, journals they wanted to found, conferences they wanted to hold, they always got what they wanted. They were never short of funds because it was a matter of life and death. Governments and businessmen would never dare throw a spanner in the works because it was understood that Sovietologists were pursuing an enormously important practical aim: saving humanity from destruction.

That was during the Cold War.

That's all well and good, but what happened? Despite all the conferences, chairs and journals, there was not a single Sovietologist who predicted what would actually happen: the peaceful collapse of the Soviet Union. That possibility was not on their radar, because Sovietologists only ever entertained two theories: the theory of convergence and the theory of mutual destruction. The theory of convergence postulated that the capitalists would learn from the communists, and the communists from the capitalists, and that the two systems would gradually converge until it would become impossible to tell them apart. We would end up with a kind of worldwide consensus. The other theory was called 'MAD', the acronym for 'mutually assured destruction' – the 'balance of terror' or 'nuclear stalemate' – a situation in which each side is so strong that any war would end with the complete destruction of both. Not a single Sovietologist was able to predict that communism would collapse because of its own absurdity and stupidity, its inability to fulfil its promises – that there would not be a clash, but a collapse. There were some imaginative writers and self-styled prophets who occasionally considered the possibility, but no one from the discipline of Sovietology. For the scientists, this scenario did not exist.

But what is true of Sovietology need not therefore hold for all attempts at predicting the future.

It does, and for logical reasons. Leszek Kołakowski put it very neatly. Futurology, he said, is one of the greatest shams in the history of thought, because it seeks to be the science of something that not only does not exist, but also cannot exist. The future, by definition, is something that does not yet exist, and once it does exist, it is no longer the future but the present. A science of the future is impossible: there cannot be a science with no subject matter. The reason is not that we are too stupid, incompetent or whatever. It is impossible in principle.

It is difficult to make predictions, especially about the future, as they say.

When I was still teaching, whenever examination time would approach and the students started to get nervous and agitated, I always set them a particular reading as a kind of therapy, to distract them and calm them down. I recommended a book on futurology that had been published twenty years ago. How that made them laugh!

But the fact that the future can't be predicted for ontological reasons does not prevent us from trying again and again.

These attempts will never be abandoned. There is an urge – one has to do it. Ernst Bloch, like many other philosophers, insisted on the fact that, as humans, we are naturally and culturally oriented towards the future. Unlike other animals, we are able to imagine something that does not exist. What's more, our language includes the word 'no', meaning that – again, unlike other animals – we can deny something that does actually exist. Animals communicate with each other, send each other signals, but all that remains tied to the present. We have the future tense in our language. We are able to talk respectably, and without making fools of ourselves, about things that do not, or do not yet, exist. The faculty of the imagination is an indispensable prerequisite for human life, and it is thanks to the future tense that we possess it. Efforts at predicting the future cannot be eliminated from human thought.

Even if they continue to fail.

It would be nice if we could accept that what is important is not the result of these efforts but the efforts themselves. They are of enormous importance in life. But it is a mistake to think that this is an undertaking that can be brought to any kind of satisfactory conclusion. The American sociologist Robert Merton gave us the concepts of the 'self-fulfilling prophecy' and the 'self-defeating prophecy'. These are, indeed, real phenomena. Our behaviour leads to certain results and makes a prophecy either true or false.

There is plenty of evidence for this: for instance, the 'Baskerville effect', named after Arthur Conan Doyle's novel The Hound of the Baskervilles. *Americans of Chinese and Japanese origin suffer fatal heart attacks with particular frequency on the fourth day of the month, because four is considered an unlucky number in those cultures – an example of a self-fulfilling prophecy. If, however, a political party predicts ahead of an election*

*that it is heading for an overwhelming victory, many
supporters may abstain from voting because the result
appears to be in the bag – a self-defeating prophecy.
Biblical prophecies, however, have an altogether different
meaning, haven't they?*

Unlike university professors, the prophets of the Bible did
not want their prophecies to come true. On the contrary,
they wanted to warn people. They wanted to fight to keep
bad things from happening. University professors are
proud when a prediction turns out to have been correct,
even if it was a pessimistic one. It means a promotion!

*You are very critical of our contemporary society, and
from time to time there are glimpses of the Marxist you
once were.*

I learned a great deal from Marx. And I am still attached
to the socialist idea that the criterion for judging a society
is whether it enables its weakest members to live a decent
life.

*On the other hand, you're also a pessimist. The power of
the new capitalism is so great that there's very little room
for an alternative. Is that not cause for despair?*

After my lectures, someone will usually raise his hand and
ask why I'm so pessimistic. It's only when I talk about the
European Union that people ask why I'm so optimistic.
Optimists believe, like Leibniz, that this is 'the best of all
possible worlds'.[27] And pessimists fear the optimists are
right. I don't belong to either of these two factions. There
is a third category, in which I count myself: the one of
hope.

What does this category rest on?

When it comes to pessimism and optimism, there are two

attitudes. The one is that of Antonio Gramsci, who said: 'In the short term, I am a pessimist; in the long term, I am an optimist.' That is very wise. Problems cannot be solved immediately, but there is still hope. In the long term, it will be solved somehow. The other attitude comes from Stuart Hall, the Jamaican-born British sociologist. He was the founder of cultural studies, a black man who contributed enormously to the development of the idea of culture, which was still practically unknown when I came to England in 1971. Back then, I had to explain to my departmental colleagues – not to my students – what it was all about. The concept of culture did not exist in academic teaching. But Stuart Hall introduced the element of culture into sociological thought. He said: 'I'm a pessimist because of intelligence, but an optimist because of will.'[28]

That's wonderful. It reminds me of Martin Luther: 'Even if I knew that tomorrow the world will go to pieces, I would still plant my apple tree.'

I don't think that there is a huge difference between the optimist and the pessimist. I simply do not believe that we live in the best of all possible worlds, and, despite everything I have experienced, I have never lost faith in an alternative, in the possibility of a better, more just world. Thus, I am neither an optimist nor a pessimist. I think of myself as a 'man who hopes'.

In her memoir of post-war Poland, Janina writes that you experienced several periods of despair: in 1953, when your military career was abruptly ended; in 1968, when you lost your chair at the University of Warsaw during the anti-Semitic purge; and then, during your first time as an emigrant in Great Britain, in London and Leeds, when you felt terribly lonely. But Janina also writes that you have 'a rare gift for turning gloom into brightness, for making small misfortunes into an occasion for happiness never to be forgotten'.[29] Where does this ability come from?

The 'rare gift for turning gloom into brightness' – well, that was Janina's view. That was what she wrote in her book. I think she meant that, for me, the fact that something fails does not prove that it is impossible. You have to carry on and try again. You make a mistake. The next time, with any luck, you will do better, and it will be better. The gift for turning gloom into brightness? Well, I do not want to abandon hope.

Were your parents the same? Your mother or your father?

My father was a wonderful man. I treasure my memories of him, for two reasons: firstly, he was extremely honest – too sincere, I would say. Because of his honesty, we almost lost our lives when fleeing from Poznań. Our train had stopped at a station because the Germans were bombarding it, and he did not want us to run away before he had found a guard and paid our fares. Secondly, he was a selfless man. He was never thinking about his own interests. He devoted himself fully to the family, and he did whatever he could to make sure that we were happy. There wasn't much that he could do – firstly, because of the situation, and secondly, because of his character, which was wholly unsuited to that situation. He was a born thinker. He was only ever happy at night. I don't know how he did it. He came home from work, but at nine o'clock, when his children and his wife had all gone to bed, he lit a candle and he read. Whatever benefits he took from it, however, he sacrificed for the care of his family. I don't think that he had any hope. He had a very deep sense of duty, and that kept him alive.

Like him, you did not despair, even when you had every reason to.

Don't forget that Janina had far more cause for despair in her life than I had. I was never in the ghetto. She was. All told, I only lived under Nazi rule for two weeks. And later, the only time I ever encountered Nazis, I had a rifle in my hands. I never experienced the despair of someone who knows she is destined for annihilation. Janina did. She was magnificent. Between 1939 and 1945, she confronted death head-on many, many times. When you read her *Winter in the Morning: A Young Girl's Life in the Warsaw Ghetto*, her memoir of those terrible years, there were moments … On one occasion, she was hiding with her mother and sister in a cellar. A group of German soldiers came in with torches, shone them in the cellar. They came closer and closer, before one of the soldiers suddenly shouted: 'Done. There's no one here.' I never lived through something like that. All my difficult moments had a happy ending.

You have a soft spot for the 'underdog', for the losers, the socially disadvantaged – especially for those who keep trying, nevertheless. Where does that come from?

Looking back, it comes from my love for the football club Polonia Warszawa. This love affair began in 1937, when the club fought bravely and successfully for promotion to the first league, before going on to beat Ruch Chorzów – the unbeatable champions of Polish football for many years – 4–0 on the champions' own turf. Around roughly the same time, I read the fable of the two frogs who fall into a bowl of milk. The first one shouts: 'I'm done! I shall drown.' And so he does. The other one says nothing but puts all his energy into a desperate attempt to remain afloat. With all four legs, he paddles tirelessly. The milk gradually turns to butter, and the frog is able to step on the butter and thus finally leap to freedom. I think the accidental coincidence of these two philosophically significant events played a formative role in my life – or, rather, in my philosophy of life. Yes, I have a soft spot for the scrappy underdog. I saw Polonia Warszawa play for the first time eleven years after I first fell in love with the team from a distance. The club has generously repaid my emotional investment. Over the years I have been a fan,

Polonia Warzawa has alternated between periods of poor form and periods of hope.

How does your 'principle of hope' – if I may use Ernst Bloch's term – fit with your admiration of Michel Houllebecq, arguably one of the most depressing contemporary authors?

I like Houellebecq because of his sharp eye and his gift for detecting the general in the specific, uncovering and extrapolating its inner potential, as in his *The Possibility of an Island*, the most insightful dystopia to date about the deregulated, fragmented and individualized society of liquid modernity. He is very sceptical and devoid of hope, and he provides many good reasons for his assessment. I do not completely agree with his position, but I find it difficult to refute his arguments. It is a dystopia that can be compared to Orwell's *1984*. Orwell wrote about the fears of his generation, while Houellebecq describes what will happen if we go on like this: the last stage of loneliness, separation and the meaninglessness of life.

What, then, of hope?

Something tremendously important is missing in Houellebecq's portrayal of the situation. The powerlessness of politics and the powerlessness of the individual are not the only culprits to blame for the bleakness of the present prospects, and, precisely because of this, the current state of affairs doesn't preclude the possibility of a reversal. Pessimism – that's passivity, doing nothing because nothing can be changed. But I'm not passive. I write books and think, and I'm passionately engaged. My role is to warn people about the dangers and to do something about them.

Happiness and Morality

The good life: what does it mean to take off shoes that are too tight?

The concept of responsibility plays an important role in your thinking. You talk about a 'responsibility for responsibility'. What do you mean by that?

Everything we do has an effect on other people's lives. We do not like to think about this. What I call taking 'responsibility for responsibility' is the moral recognition of this objectively given responsibility.

That means that, in all our decisions, we are confronted with a choice between right and wrong, good and evil?

Even before we know what good and evil are, we are faced with this choice in the very moment we meet the other. We are inescapably and existentially moral beings, charged with taking responsibility for our fellow human beings. This choice involves us in an ambivalent situation. The moral life is a life of continuous uncertainty. To be moral means to take responsibility for one's own responsibility.

*How does the way modernity deals with this ambivalence
differ from the way it was dealt with in earlier times?*

In the premodern era, this burden was mostly dealt
with through religion. The burden of having made the
wrong decision was retrospectively eased by the seeking
of absolution for the sin committed. The modern project
of remodelling the world according to a rational plan, by
contrast, promised a life free of sin. The world was meant
not only to be free of sinners, but to be free of sin itself.
Its place was taken by guilt. And the authority in charge
of that was the legislature.

*And how do the ethics of modernity differ from the ethics
of postmodernity – or 'liquid modernity', as you would
put it?*

In traditional ethics, you had to follow the rules.
Postmodern morality, by contrast, demands that everyone
take responsibility for their own behaviour. The human
being becomes a vagabond, deciding for him- or herself
what is good and evil. That would be fine if interpersonal
relations were not now so shaped by consumerism.

*Two ethical thinkers who have influenced your thinking,
the Danish philosopher and theologian Knud Løgstrup and
the French-Lithuanian philosopher Emmanuel Levinas,
give accounts of moral action. Løgstrup says it presupposes 'spontaneity', an absence of premeditation. For
Levinas, if one were to ask why one should act morally,
this would spell the end of moral action. Is it wrong to
ask about the necessity, or even just the advisability, of
morality?*

That is what those two are saying. Acting morally, being
there for the other, never serves a purpose. It is not about
hoping to gain a profit, or to be admired or publicly
acclaimed. When it comes to moral questions, there is no

'must'; moral action presupposes the freely taken decision of the individual. An act is moral only if it is not calculative – if it is done spontaneously and without thinking, as an act of humanity. The knowledge that one may make right and wrong decisions is the soil in which morality grows.

So morality does not emerge from a feeling of duty. It is innate.

Levinas says that the questions 'Why should I act morally?', 'What has anyone else done for me?' and 'Why should I do this if no one else does?' mark not the beginning but the end of moral action. Løgstrup says that, even if some rule tells you to do something because it is good, following the rule does not constitute moral behaviour. Moral action presupposes a free decision. It is about caring, being there for the other – the impulse to help the other without thinking about it. Knud Løgstrup was the priest of a small parish on the island of Funen before becoming a professor of ethics and the philosophy of religion at the University of Aarhus. Emmanuel Levinas taught at the Sorbonne in Paris. It is mysterious that these two men, who set out from very different starting points, lived far apart from each other, and did not read each other's work, developed the very same ideas. In physics, that is normal. Physicists study the material world, and if someone does not make a discovery, then sooner or later someone else will.

Someone else would have come up with the theory of relativity even if Einstein had not done so. That is the case in all of the so-called hard sciences.

But in the humanities, this is not the case. Every discovery is really an individual achievement. Someone else may happen upon that discovery by chance, but not necessarily, not as the result of a law. But Levinas and Løgstrup reached the same conclusion. Levinas articulated it in terms of responsibility, and Løgstrup in terms of 'silent demands'. The idea is the same – it is only expressed in different terms. And it is very interesting when you think about it. Løgstrup says that Jesus could not have developed a Christian ethics, because a Christian ethics would have produced educated conformists and not moral individuals. Morality is not about following a rule book but about reacting to an unknown and silent demand. It is the responsibility of the one called upon to decipher the message. The demand is not articulated, nor do we have to respond to it. And if we do something, we will never be certain, in retrospect, that we have done all that needed to be done. We will not even know if what we did was the right thing to do, or if we were up to the task. Morality is part of the realm of uncertainty. This position stands in opposition to the views of most moral philosophers, who see morality as an organ of certainty. Neither Levinas nor Løgstrup has any hope that we can achieve certainty regarding moral questions.

Morality is a burden.

It is not a recipe for happiness. It is a recipe for a difficult life. Morality is an unfinished process; there is no resting point. The natural state of the moral person is one of perpetual uncertainty.

This understanding of ethics differs from that of Kant, whose categorical imperative provides a clear guideline for how to act: 'So act that the maxim of your will could always hold at the same time as a principle in a giving of universal law.'[30] *That is relatively simple. It does not threaten to plunge you into a state of despair and permanent inadequacy. Doesn't what Levinas and Løgstrup say amount to an unreasonable demand?*

I do not believe that uncertainty is a threat to morality. On the contrary, it is the only fertile soil in which it can grow. And it is precisely the loneliness of this uncertainty that provides a hope for moral community. Everyone is left to their own devices and must bear individual responsibility. The absence of compulsion, the uncertainty of the situation, gives rise to right decisions and wrong decisions. There is no guarantee that the right decision will be made, but there is hope.

What can sociology tell us about why human beings make particular decisions in moral situations?

In her study *When Light Pierced the Darkness*, the Polish sociologist Nechama Tec investigated the motivations of individual Christians who risked their lives to save Jews from annihilation. To her own surprise, and to the surprise of all experts, she could not find any statistically significant factor underlying moral action. There is no connection between the willingness to help, to make sacrifices, and class membership, income, education, religion or political orientation. Why different people behave differently in the same situation remains a mystery. At the end of the day, it is down to personality and responsibility.

In today's 'global village' media world, we witness so much avoidable misery, hunger, sickness and death that it is hard to know where to begin.

The philosopher Hans Jonas has written about how to do the right thing on a global level. If we have prophets of doom on the one hand, and optimists who believe we live in the best of all possible worlds on the other, Jonas says, then we should trust the prophets of doom. We cannot know the consequences of our acts and omissions, but we are responsible for them. What someone does in Berlin may have unforeseen effects on the future of Bangladesh. The same applies to us here and now. Whatever we do determines the living conditions of our as-yet-unborn grandchildren. They are not yet on this earth, but by using up the planet's resources we are already influencing their lives. We are limiting their freedom. Today, the consequences of our actions reach further beyond ourselves than ever before. In previous times, we know from ethnology, the earth's inhabitants made small changes that influenced their immediate present and immediate future. About 100,000 years ago, the needle was invented. Do you know how long it took before someone had the idea of drilling a hole in the end of the needle in order to attach a thread to it?

No.

30,000 years! It took a long time. In some way or other, the people of the Palaeolithic also influenced the future without knowing it. But that cannot be compared to our situation today.

In your book The Art of Life, *you talk about happiness, a subject addressed by the philosophers of antiquity. In modernity, happiness has become a thing to be chased after.*

It started with the American Declaration of Independence in 1776, which proclaims 'life, liberty and the pursuit of happiness' as inalienable, God-given human rights. Of course, human beings have always preferred to be happy, rather than unhappy. Evolution has endowed us with a drive to pursue happiness. Otherwise, we would still be sitting in caves instead of these comfortable armchairs. But the idea that each and every one of us has the right to pursue it in our own way has only existed since modernity. The proclamation of a general human right to individual happiness marked the start of modernity.

But it seems no less difficult to attain happiness today than it was during Roman times, the era of Seneca's, Lucretius', Marcus Aurelius' and Epictetus' philosophies of life. What does happiness mean to you personally?

When Goethe was around my age, he was asked if he had had a happy life. He responded, 'Yes, I have had a very happy life, but I can't think of a single happy week.' This is a very wise answer. I feel exactly the same way. In one of his poems, Goethe also said that there isn't anything more depressing than a long stretch of sunny days.[31] Happiness isn't the alternative to life's struggles and difficulties. The alternative to that is boredom. If there aren't any problems to be solved, no challenges to be met that occasionally exceed our capabilities, we become bored. And boredom is one of the most widespread human afflictions. Happiness – and here I agree with Sigmund Freud – is not a state but a moment, an instant. We feel happy when we overcome adversity. We take off a pair of tight shoes that pinch our feet, and we feel relieved and happy. Continuous happiness is dreadful, a nightmare.

The British economist Richard Layard uses the results of happiness research in his work on economics. In his book Happiness, *he shows that an increase in income only partially helps to increase our feelings of happiness. What, then, can we do to increase our happiness?*

Work hard. A painter who creates a work of art, a mathematician who grapples with a difficult problem, a gardener who plants something and watches it bloom – that is happiness. You have created something. At the beginning of the twentieth century, the American sociologist Thorstein Veblen introduced the term 'workmanship' for the desire to do a solid job. The pride in good work, getting to grips with a task, overcoming a seemingly insurmountable obstacle – these make us happy. Everyone has this deep inside themselves. Today, we have lost the sense of joy in our own work, the feeling of pleasure in having done something well. And with that, we have lost self-confidence and the ability to enjoy a feeling of happiness. Research suggests that about half of what is essential for our contentment cannot be commercialized, and therefore cannot be bought in a shop. As long as we equate being happy with the purchase of new goods that promise happiness, the search for happiness will be endless. The closer we get to the goal, the more it loses its power to attract us and to make us happy, which is why it must continually be replaced.

If you are chasing this kind of happiness, you are first and foremost concerned with your own well-being. But it is also possible to look after the well-being of others.

Yes, and that is what ultimately makes us happy. But the pursuit of one's own happiness and that of other people's happiness are not mutually exclusive. The contradiction between selfishness and altruism can be resolved. If you only look to your own self-interest, you do not need to care about the well-being of others. But caring about others also makes you feel better yourself. The former is Nietzsche's project. He goes in for selfishness, self-realization and self-advancement. Levinas turns, no less radically, towards the other – towards care for the other and the happiness one derives from being there for the other.

We are all experts in the art of living, you say. What is the art of living?

Attempting the impossible. Understanding ourselves as the product of our own doing and creating. Setting ourselves tasks that we can hardly accomplish, like a painter or sculptor. Pursuing goals that exceed our own possibilities at the moment. Judging all the things we do – or could do – according to standards that lie above our present capabilities. I cannot repeat it often enough: uncertainty is our natural habitat – even if the hope of transforming it into the opposite is the driving force behind our pursuit of happiness.

You not only provided a theory of the transition from 'solid' to 'liquid' modernity, but you also experienced it first-hand. What did you want when you were young?

As a young man, like many of my contemporaries, I was influenced by Sartre's idea of a 'projet de la vie'. Create your own plan for your life and move towards this ideal, taking the shortest and most direct path. Decide what kind of person you want to be, and then you have the formula for becoming this person. For each kind of life, there are a certain number of rules you have to follow, a number of characteristics you must acquire. Life, as Sartre sees it, proceeds step by step along a route that is determined, from beginning to end, before we embark on the journey.

That is the secular equivalent of the Christian path to salvation.

Yes, and the assumption, as in the case of the Christian path to salvation, was that things will always have the same value as they have now. The world will remain stable. Advice about which characteristics one should acquire and how to acquire them are valid at age 8, and they will be valid at age 50. You begin an apprenticeship at 16 or 18, and you know that, forty years later, you will retire from the same company with a pension. That sounds absurd to young people today. They know that every job is only for the time being, that everyone is employed on a temporary basis, and that you will change jobs fifteen to twenty times during your lifetime.

As you mentioned, the big change took place in the seventies, when the post-war Wirtschaftswunder, *or* Les Trente Glorieuses – *the three decades of reconstruction, social peace and optimism after the war – came to an end. This was an exceptional period in the history of capitalism, as Thomas Piketty has shown in his global bestseller* Capital in the Twenty-First Century.

This cleared the way for the brave new world of information overload, unbridled deregulation and frenzied consumerism in the rich North, and despair and exclusion in large parts of the rest of the world. In retrospect, we can recognize the 1970s as the decisive turning point in the history of the modern era. By the end of that decade, the context in which women and men confront the challenges of life had changed radically. Worldly wisdoms that had stood the test of time were revealed as no longer valid, and long-established life strategies had to be thoroughly revised.

What remained stable?

The only entity with an increasing life expectancy today is the individual, whereas political parties, political movements, institutions, banks, factories go through frequent changes. Their life expectancy is shrinking. We are now stable, but we inhabit a permanently changing environment. In my view, this has led to a completely different understanding of life.

You experienced the totalitarian regimes of the twentieth century, National Socialism and communism, then post-communist Eastern Europe, and now the multicultural, postmodern capitalist society of Great Britain. What makes for a good society?

I no longer believe that there is such a thing as a good society. A good society would be one that says to itself: 'We are not good enough.'

Translator's notes

1 Isaiah Berlin, *The Hedgehog and the Fox: An Essay on Tolstoy's View of History* (London: Orion Books, 1992), p. 3.
2 The reference is to the Internal Security Corps mentioned above.
3 Janina Bauman, *A Dream of Belonging: My Years in Postwar Poland* (London: Virago, 1988), p. 109.
4 Leszek Kołakowski, 'The Death of Gods', in *Is God Happy? Collected Essays* (New York: Basic Books, 2013), pp. 5–19; here, p. 5.
5 Karl Marx, *The Eighteenth Brumaire of Louis Bonaparte* (New York: International Publishers, 1963), p. 32.
6 Wiesław Myśliwski, *Ostatnie Rozdanie* [Last deal] (Cracow: Znak, 2013).
7 *Los Angeles Review of Books*, 11 November 2014; https://lareviewofbooks.org/article/disconnecting-acts-interview-zygmunt-bauman-part.
8 See 'Extract from the Speech by Adolf Hitler, January 30, 1939', available at www.yadvashem.org/docs/extract-from-hitler-speech.html.
9 See George Orwell, 'Why I Write', available at www.orwellfoundation.com/the-orwell-foundation/orwell/essays-and-other-works/why-i-write.

10 Ibid.

11 Ibid.

12 Zygmunt Bauman, *This Is Not a Diary* (Cambridge: Polity, 2012), p. 1.

13 See Romans 11:33 (King James Version).

14 See Carl Schmitt, *Political Theology: Four Chapters on the Concept of Sovereignty* (University of Chicago Press, 2005). The text was originally published in 1922; the translation is of the revised edition of 1934. In 1970, Schmitt published *Politische Theologie II: Die Legende von der Erledigung jeder Politischen Theologie* (*Political Theology II: The Myth of the Closure of any Political Theology*, Cambridge: Polity, 2008), but Bauman clearly refers to the pre-war text.

15 Richard Sennett, *The Fall of Public Man* (London: Penguin, 2003 [1977]), p. 264.

16 See Job 1:21 (KJV).

17 Benjamin Disraeli, *Sybil, or the Two Nations* (Oxford University Press, 1998), p. 66; quoted by Bauman in *Retrotopia* (Cambridge: Polity, 2017), p. 86.

18 Bauman, *Retrotopia*, p. 88.

19 Ibid., p. 89.

20 J. M. Coetzee, *Diary of a Bad Year* (London: Vintage, 2008), p. 12.

21 Cf. also *Retrotopia*, pp. 155ff.

22 Revelation 21:5 (KJV).

23 The quotation is not actually from Socrates (or Plato), but from Kenneth John Freeman, who, in his Cambridge dissertation of 1907, *Schools of Hellas: An Essay on the Practice and Theory of Ancient Greek Education from 600 to 300 B.C.* (London: Macmillan, 1907, p. 74), summed up the views of the youth in ancient Greece thus: 'The counts of the indictment are luxury, bad manners, contempt for authority, disrespect to elders, and a love for chatter in place of exercise.' These lines captured the imagination of many a reader, and the misattribution to Socrates has a long history. For details, see https://quoteinvestigator.com/2010/05/01/misbehave.

24 Leszek Kołakowski, *Main Currents of Marxism* (New York: W. W. Norton & Company Inc., 2005), p. 1212. Haffner quotes from the German edition of Kołakowski's book which has 'Unzulänglichkeit' [inadequacy] instead of 'bondage'.

25 Harald Welzer, *Climate Wars: Why People Will be Killed in the Twenty-First Century* (Cambridge: Polity, 2012).

26 Zygmunt Bauman, *Wasted Lives: Modernity and Its Outcasts* (Cambridge: Polity, 2004), p. 5.

27 Gottfried Wilhelm Leibniz, *Theodicy: Essays on the Goodness of God, the Freedom of Man and the Origin of Evil* (Withorn: Anodos Books, 2017), p. 149.

28 The phrase is usually attributed to Antonio Gramsci, who, in his 1920 'An Address to the Anarchists' in *L'Ordine nuovo*, adopted it from Romain Rolland (see https://libcom.org/history/address-anarchists-antonio-gramsci-1920: 'The Socialist concept of the revolutionary process is characterised by two basic features which Romain Rolland has summed up in his watchword: "Pessimism of the intellect, optimism of the will"'). The formulation quoted here is used by Gramsci in a letter of 19 December 1929 (*Letters from Prison*, New York: Columbia University Press, 1994, p. 299; see also the very informative fn. 1, p. 300). Stuart Hall, in turn, adopted the motto from Gramsci.

29 Janina Bauman, *A Dream of Belonging: My Years in Postwar Poland* (London: Virago, 1988), p. 165.

30 Immanuel Kant, *Critique of Practical Reason* (Cambridge University Press, 2015), p. 28.

31 'Alles in der Welt läßt sich ertragen, / Nur nicht eine Reihe von schönen Tagen.' 'All things in the world can be withstood / Except a string of days sublime and good': Johann Wolfgang Goethe, *Proverbs* (Morrisville: Lulu Press, 2014), p. 21.

Select bibliography

Zygmunt Bauman

Legislators and Interpreters: On Modernity, Post-Modernity and Intellectuals, Cambridge: Polity, 1991.
Modernity and the Holocaust, Ithaca, NY: Cornell University Press, 1989.
Thinking Sociologically: An Introduction for Everyone, Oxford: Basil Blackwell, 1990.
Modernity and Ambivalence, Cambridge: Polity, 1993.
Intimations of Postmodernity, London: Routledge, 1992.
Mortality, Immortality and Other Life Strategies, Cambridge: Polity, 1992.
Postmodern Ethics, Oxford: Basil Blackwell, 1993.
Life in Fragments: Essays in Postmodern Morality, Oxford: Basil Blackwell, 1995.
Alone Again: Ethics After Certainty, London: Demos, 1996.
Postmodernity and its Discontents, Cambridge: Polity, 1997.
Globalization: The Human Consequences, Cambridge: Polity, 1998.
In Search of Politics, Cambridge: Polity, 1999.
Liquid Modernity, Cambridge: Polity, 2000.
Community: Seeking Safety in an Insecure World, Cambridge: Polity, 2000.

Liquid Love: On the Frailty of Human Bonds, Cambridge: Polity, 2003.
Wasted Lives: Modernity and its Outcasts, Cambridge: Polity, 2004.
Liquid Life, Cambridge: Polity, 2005.
Liquid Fear, Cambridge: Polity, 2006.
Liquid Times: Living in an Age of Uncertainty, Cambridge: Polity, 2007.
Consuming Life, Cambridge: Polity, 2007.
The Art of Life, Cambridge: Polity, 2008.
Liquid Surveillance, Zygmunt Bauman and David Lyon, Cambridge: Polity, 2012.
Of God and Man, Zygmunt Bauman and Stanisław Obirek, Cambridge: Polity, 2015.
On the World and Ourselves, Zygmunt Bauman and Stanisław Obirek, Cambridge: Polity, 2015.
Strangers at Our Door, Cambridge: Polity, 2016.
Retrotopia, Cambridge: Polity, 2017.

Janina Bauman

Winter in the Morning: A Young Girl's Life in the Warsaw Ghetto, London: Virago, 1986.
A Dream of Belonging: My Years in Postwar Poland, London: Virago, 1988.